Table of Contents

Getting Started

Unit 1 At Home

Unit 6 Life Science

Unit 7 Physical Science

Unit 8   Earth and Space Science

Unit 9   Math

Numbers

Label.

eighteen	eleven	five	fifteen	four
thirteen	seven	twelve	twenty	two

1   2   3   4

1.   one   _____   three   _____

5   6   7   8

2.   _____   six   _____   eight

9   10   11   12

3.   nine   ten   _____   _____

13   14   15   16

4.   _____   fourteen   _____   sixteen

17   18   19   20

5.   seventeen   _____   nineteen   _____

1. eighty-   100

2. twenty-three   29

3. one hundred   96

4. eighty-eight   23

5. twenty-four   24

6. twenty-nine   80

7. ninety-six   88

8. twenty-five   25

C Label.

| thirty | seventy | fifty |

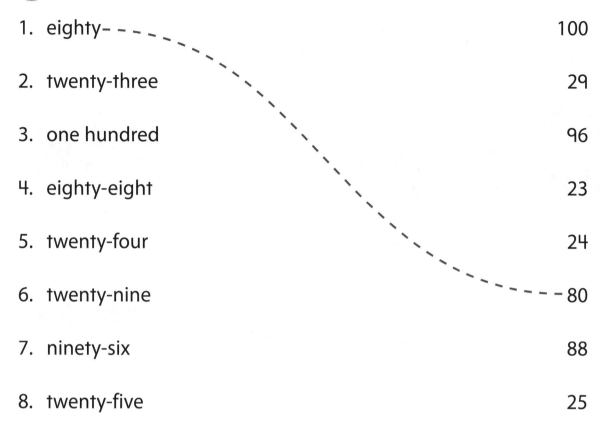

1. _____   2. _____   3. _____

Ordinal Numbers

A Label.

fifth	tenth	first	fourth	second	eighth

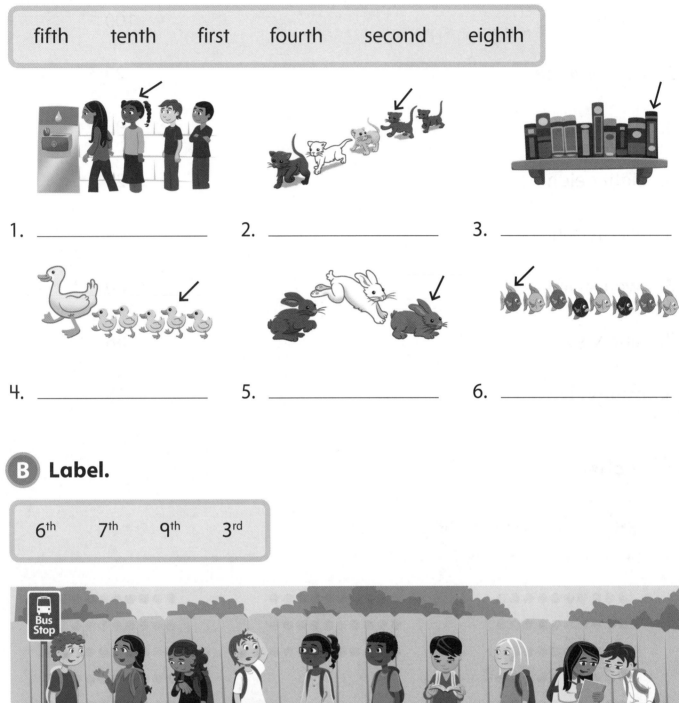

1. _____

2. _____

3. _____

4. _____

5. _____

6. _____

B Label.

6th	7th	9th	3rd

1st   2nd _____   4th   5th _____ _____ 8th _____ 10th

Calendar

A **Label.**

December	July	May	March	January	October

_____

1	2	3	4	5	6	7
8	9	10	11	12	13	14
15	16	17	18	19	20	21
22	23	24	25	26	27	28
29	30	31

February

			1	2	3	4
5	6	7	8	9	10	11
12	13	14	15	16	17	18
19	20	21	22	23	24	25
26	27	28	29

_____

				1	2	3
4	5	6	7	8	9	10
11	12	13	14	15	16	17
18	19	20	21	22	23	24
25	26	27	28	29	30	31

April

1	2	3	4	5	6	7
8	9	10	11	12	13	14
15	16	17	18	19	20	21
22	23	24	25	26	27	28
29	30

_____

		1	2	3	4	5
6	7	8	9	10	11	12
13	14	15	16	17	18	19
20	21	22	23	24	25	26
27	28	29	30	31

June

					1	2
3	4	5	6	7	8	9
10	11	12	13	14	15	16
17	18	19	20	21	22	23
24	25	26	27	28	29	30

_____

1	2	3	4	5	6	7
8	9	10	11	12	13	14
15	16	17	18	19	20	21
22	23	24	25	26	27	28
29	30	31

August

				1	2	3	4
5	6	7	8	9	10	11
12	13	14	15	16	17	18
19	20	21	22	23	24	25
26	27	28	29	30	31

September

						1
2	3	4	5	6	7	8
9	10	11	12	13	14	15
16	17	18	19	20	21	22
23	24	25	26	27	28	29
30

_____

	1	2	3	4	5	6
7	8	9	10	11	12	13
14	15	16	17	18	19	20
21	22	23	24	25	26	27
28	29	30	31

November

				1	2	3
4	5	6	7	8	9	10
11	12	13	14	15	16	17
18	19	20	21	22	23	24
25	26	27	28	29	30

_____

						1
2	3	4	5	6	7	8
9	10	11	12	13	14	15
16	17	18	19	20	21	22
23	24	25	26	27	28	29
30	31

B **Write the days in the correct order.**

Thursday	Wednesday	Friday	Monday	Saturday	Tuesday

1. Sunday _____

2. _____

3. _____

4. _____

5. _____

6. _____

7. _____

Time

A Label.

| afternoon | evening | midnight | morning | night | noon |

1. _____

2. _____

3. _____

4. _____

5. _____

6. _____

6

Colors

Color.

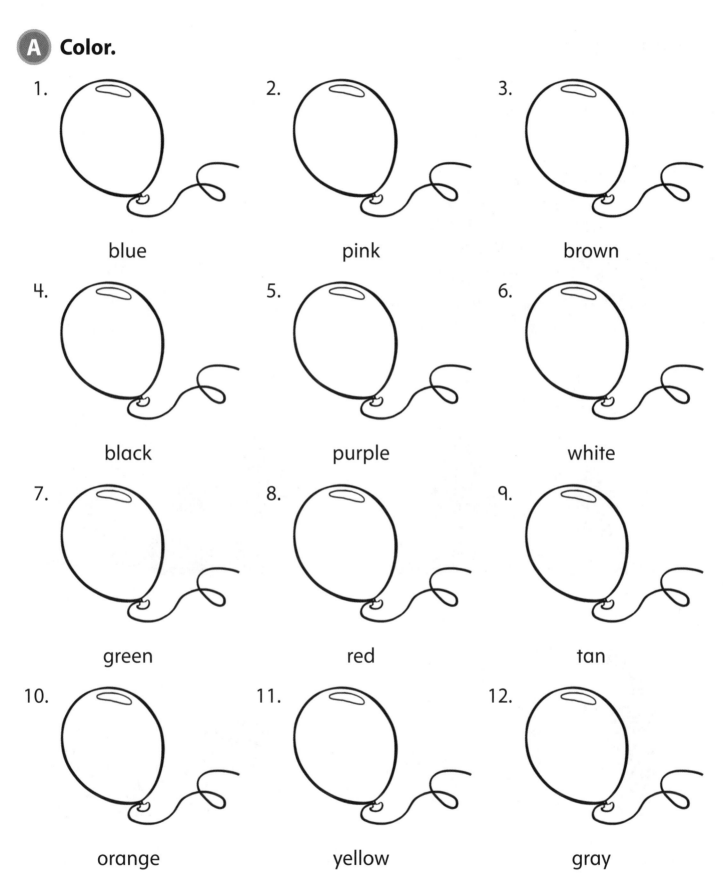

1. blue

2. pink

3. brown

4. black

5. purple

6. white

7. green

8. red

9. tan

10. orange

11. yellow

12. gray

7

Opposites

A Label.

| fast | left | new | open | small | tall |

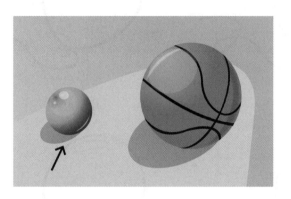

1. _____

2. _____

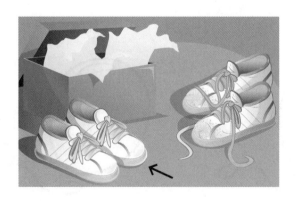

3. _____

4. _____

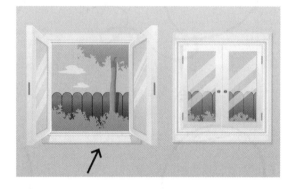

5. _____

6. _____

Write.

| cold | different | dirty | empty | heavy | wet |

1. Full is the opposite of _____.

2. Light is the opposite of _____.

3. Clean is the opposite of _____.

4. Dry is the opposite of _____.

5. Hot is the opposite of _____.

6. Same is the opposite of _____.

Prepositions

Circle.

1. The book is (between) the boxes.
   next to

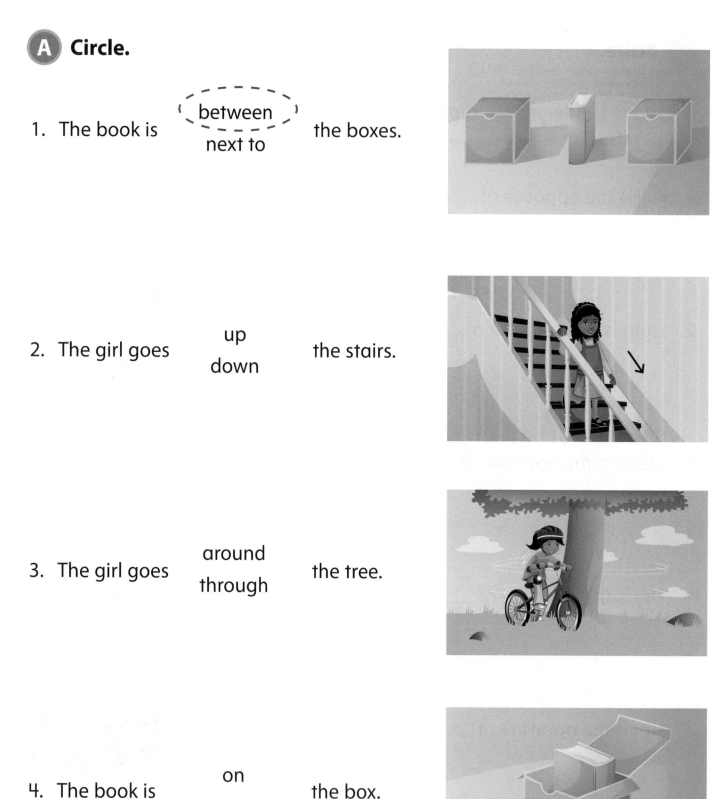

2. The girl goes up the stairs.
   down

3. The girl goes around the tree.
   through

4. The book is on the box.
   in

10

B **Write.**

| above | behind | across from | in front of | over | below | under |

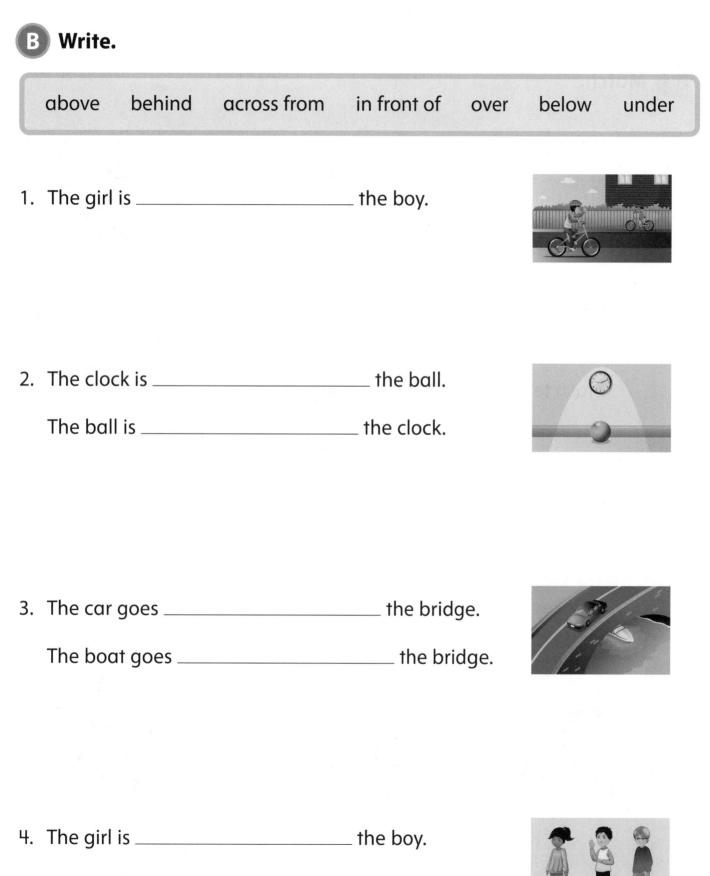

1. The girl is _____ the boy.

2. The clock is _____ the ball.

   The ball is _____ the clock.

3. The car goes _____ the bridge.

   The boat goes _____ the bridge.

4. The girl is _____ the boy.

   The boy is _____ the girl.

A Match.

1. _____ comb hair

2. _____ get dressed

3. _____ eat breakfast

4. _____ brush teeth

a.

b.

c.

d.

B Write.

| eats | takes | wakes |

1. He _____ up.

2. He _____ a shower

3. She _____ dinner.

C Write.

takes a bath   does homework   goes to bed

1. She _____ at 6:30 p.m.

2. He _____ at 7:30 p.m.

3. She _____ at 8:00 p.m.

D Look at the pictures. Write.

1. She _____ up at 7:00 a.m.

2. She _____.

3. _____.

2 Friends

A Match.

1. _____ bangs
2. _____ glasses
3. _____ eyelashes
4. _____ ponytail
5. _____ eye
6. _____ hair

B Match.

dark   short   straight   long   curly   light

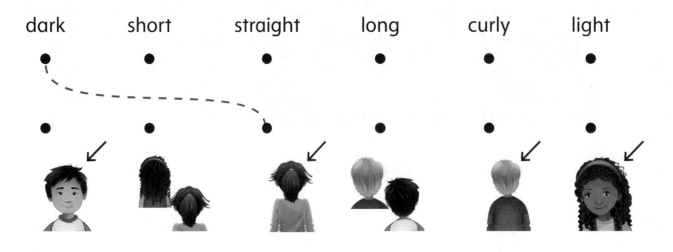

C Write.

1. She has _____ eyes.

2. He has short, _____ hair.

3. She has _____, curly hair.

D Look at the picture. Write.

1. Emma has long, _____ hair.

2. Ted has _____, _____.

3. Mary _____.

A Label.

grandmother	grandfather	mother	father
sister	brother	aunt	uncle

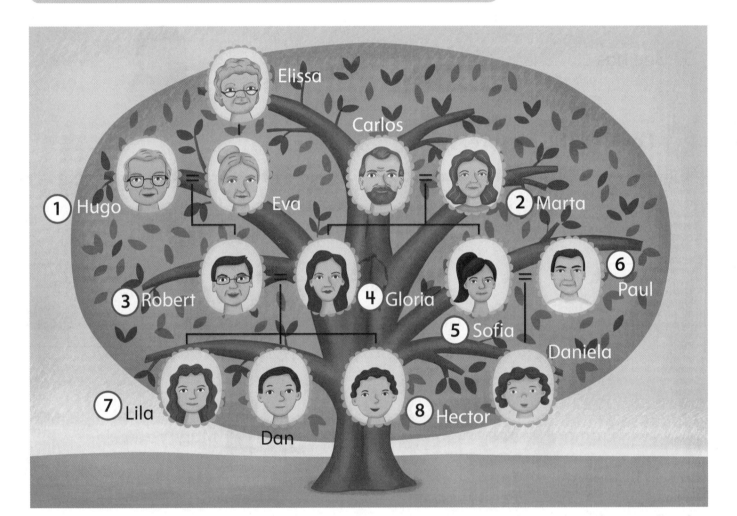

1. _____   5. _____

2. _____   6. _____

3. _____   7. _____

4. _____   8. _____

B **Look at Dan's family tree on page 16. Write.**

| parents | cousin | great-grandmother | grandparents |

1. Daniela is his _____.

2. Elissa is his _____.

3. Hugo and Eva are his _____.

4. Gloria and Robert are his _____.

C **Look at the picture. Write.**

1. Lila is Dan's _____.

2. Carlos and Marta are his _____.

3. Sofia and Paul _____.

A Match.

1. _____ cook
2. _____ wall
3. _____ eat
4. _____ floor
5. _____ stairs

6. _____ window
7. _____ table
8. _____ sink
9. _____ door
10. _____ cabinet

B **Write.**

1. There is a _____.

2. There are two _____.

3. There are three _____.

C **Look at the picture. Write.**

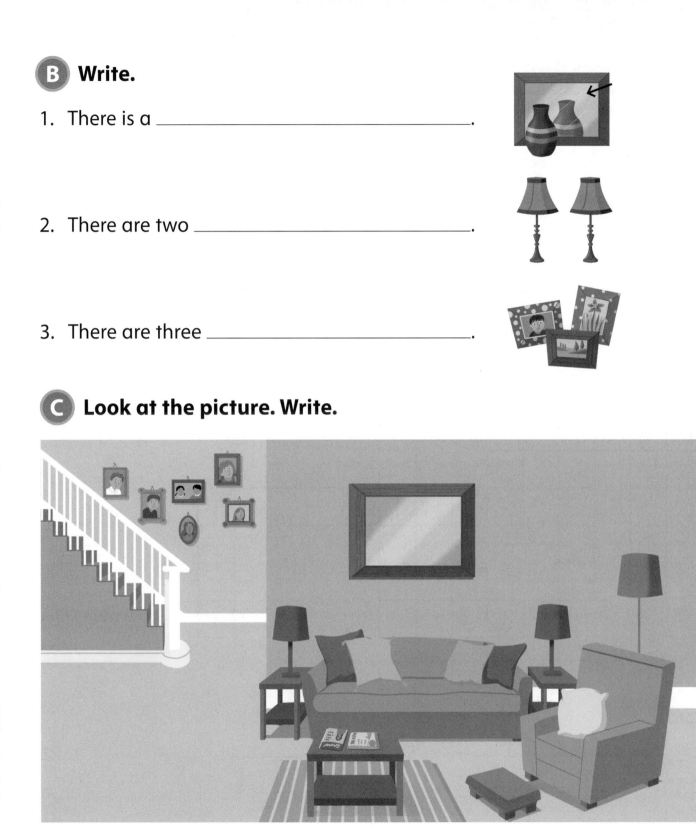

1. There _____ stairs.

2. There are three _____.

3. There _____.

19

5 The Bedroom

A Write.

Across

1. 2. 3. 4. 5.

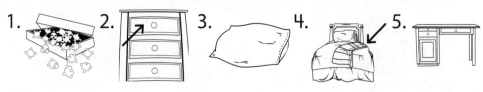

Down

6. 7. 8. 9. 10. 11. 12.

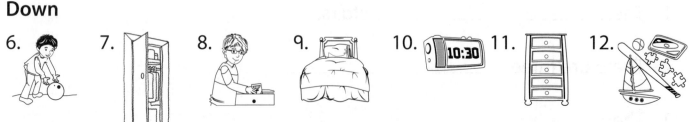

20

B **Write *in, on,* or *under*.**

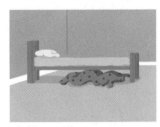

1. The puzzle is _____ the drawer.

2. The blanket is _____ the bed.

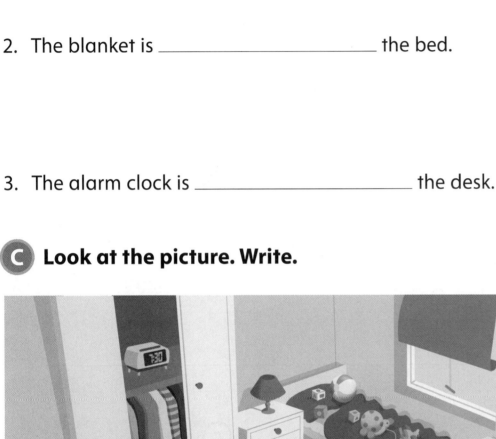

3. The alarm clock is _____ the desk.

C **Look at the picture. Write.**

1. The toys are on the _____.

2. The puzzle _____.

3. The alarm clock _____.

6 The Bathroom

A Write.

1. c_____ _____ _____

2. t_____ _____ _____ _____

3. _____ _____ _____ _____ _____paste

4. tooth_____ _____ _____ _____ _____

B Match.

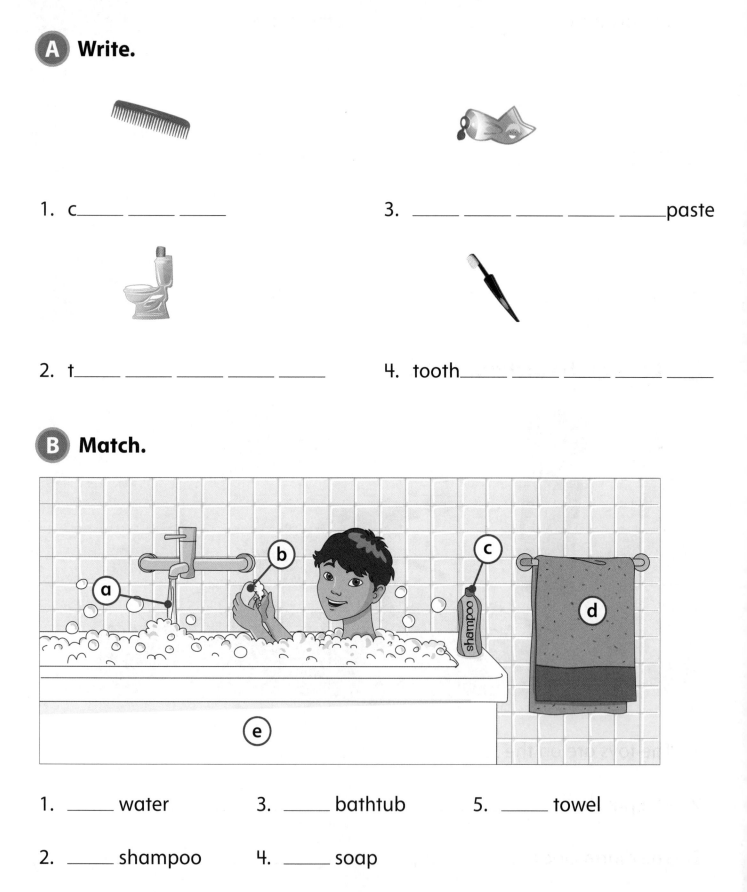

1. _____ water

2. _____ shampoo

3. _____ bathtub

4. _____ soap

5. _____ towel

C Write.

> washes   brushes   dries

1. She _____ her hands with a towel.

2. He _____ his hands with soap.

3. She _____ her teeth with a toothbrush.

D Look at the pictures. Write.

1. Tom washes his hair with _____.

2. He dries his hair with a _____.

3. _____.

7 Breakfast in the Kitchen

A Match.

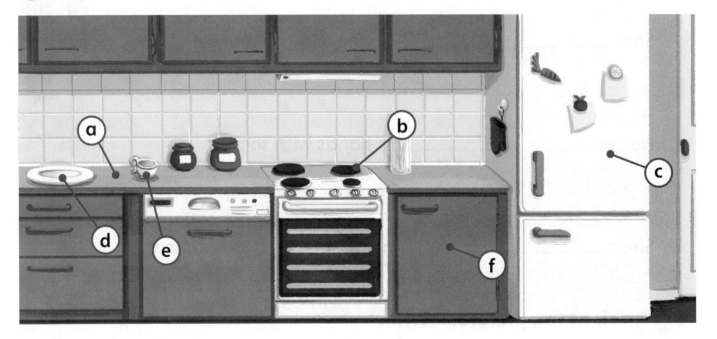

1. _____ stove

2. _____ cabinet

3. _____ refrigerator

4. _____ cup

5. _____ counter

6. _____ plate

B Match.

butter   cereal   eggs   bananas   bread   grapes

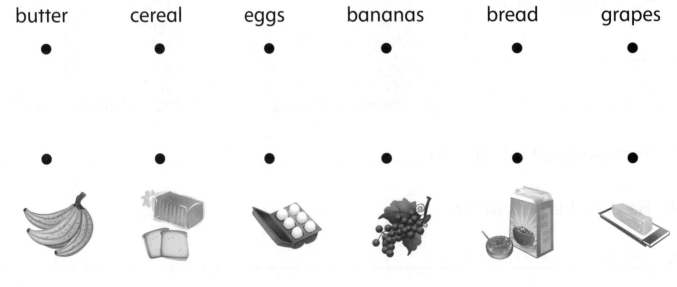

C Write.

1. Where is the _____?

   It's on the table.

2. Where are the _____?

   They're on the plate.

3. Where are the _____?

   They're on the counter.

D Look at the picture. Write.

1. The milk is on the _____.

2. The bread is _____.

3. The cereal _____.

A Circle the correct word.

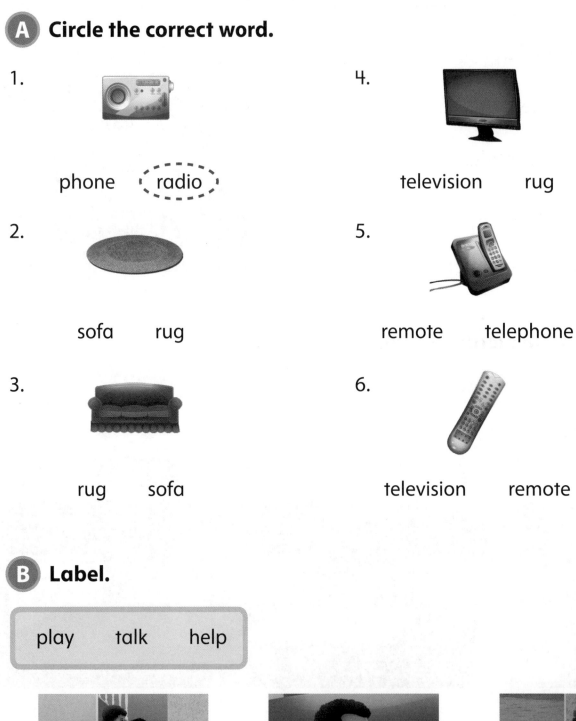

1.
phone   (radio)

2.
sofa   rug

3.
rug   sofa

4.
television   rug

5.
remote   telephone

6.
television   remote

B Label.

| play | talk | help |

1. _____   2. _____   3. _____

C Write.

helping	talking	studying

1. He's _____ the boy.

2. She's _____.

3. He's _____ on the phone.

D Look at the picture. Write.

1. They're _____ a game.

2. He's _____.

3. He's _____.

Everyday Clothes

A Match.

1. _____ pants

2. _____ sneakers

3. _____ underwear

4. _____ baseball cap

5. _____ skirt

6. _____ shoes

7. _____ dress

8. _____ socks

9. _____ sweatshirt

10. _____ pajamas

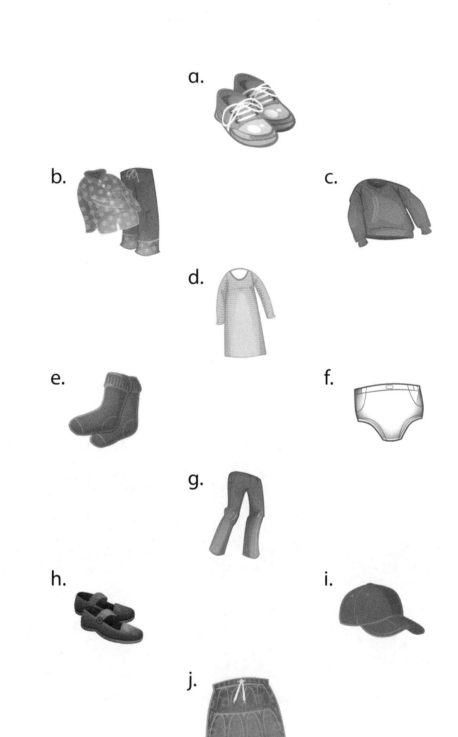

a.

b.

c.

d.

e.

f.

g.

h.

i.

j.

B Write. Then color.

1. What color is the _____?

   It's red.

2. What color are the _____?

   They're blue.

3. What color is the _____?

   It's yellow.

C Color the picture. Then write.

1. The socks are _____.

2. The sweatshirt is _____.

3. _____.

A Label.

jacket	umbrella	bathing suit	sandals	scarf	gloves
T-shirt	pants	shorts	sunglasses	raincoat	boots

Spring	Summer	Fall	Winter

B Write.

1. He's wearing _____

   and a _____.

2. She's wearing a _____

   and _____.

3. They're wearing _____.

C Look at the picture. Write.

1. They're wearing rain _____.

2. They're wearing _____.

3. _____.

A Match.

1. _____ bed

a.

b.

2. _____ refrigerator

c.

3. _____ sink

4. _____ sofa

d.

e.

5. _____ window

B Look at the chart on page 32 in the *Dictionary*. Write.

1. There is a _____ and a window in the bedroom.

2. There is a _____ and a window in the living room.

3. There is a _____ and a _____

   in the bathroom.

4. There is a _____, _____, and a

   _____ in the kitchen.

Complete the chart.

The Home		kitchen	living room	bedroom	bathroom
table		X			
dresser					
shower					
stove					
mirror					

D **Look at your chart in C. Write.**

1. There is a dresser in the _____.

2. There is a shower and a _____ in

   the _____.

3. There is a _____ and a _____

   _____.

4. _____

   _____.

11 A Day at School

A Label.

raise	read	write	draw
repeat	work	answer	think

1. _____

2. _____

3. _____

4. _____ questions

5. _____

6. _____

7. _____ hand

8. _____ with a partner

Write.

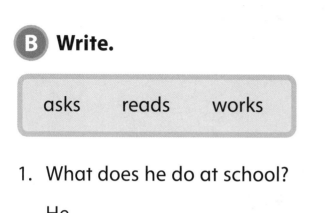

| asks | reads | works |

1. What does he do at school?

   He _____.

2. What does she do at school?

   She _____ questions.

3. What does he do at school?

   He _____ in a group.

C **Look at the picture. Write.**

Carlos   Jun   Amy

1. Carlos _____ at school.

2. Jun listens and _____.

3. Amy _____.

A Write.

1. __l__ ibrarian

2. ___ afeteria worker

3. t ___ ___ ___ ___ ___ ___

4. ___ ___ ___ driver

5. ___ ecretary

6. ___ ___ ossing guard

7. c ___ ___ ___ ___ ___ ___ ___

8. n ___ ___ ___ ___

B Answer the questions.

principal	classroom	student
office	teacher's aide	

1. Where is the _____?

   She's in the classroom.

2. Where is the _____?

   She's in the _____.

3. Where are the teacher and the _____?

   They're in the _____.

C Look at the pictures. Write.

1. The cafeteria worker is in the _____.

2. The students are _____.

3. The coach _____.

A Match.

1. _____ crayon

2. _____ pencil

3. _____ eraser

4. _____ pen

5. _____ pencil sharpener

6. _____ calculator

7. _____ book

8. _____ binder

9. _____ scissors

10. _____ marker

11. _____ backpack

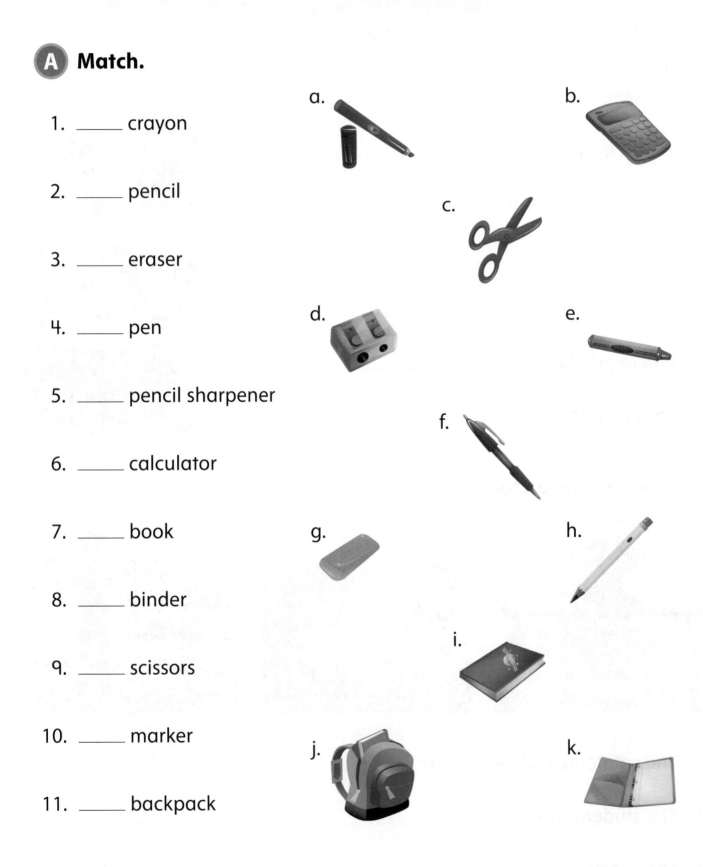

a.

b.

c.

d.

e.

f.

g.

h.

i.

j.

k.

B Write.

1. He has two _____.

2. She has three _____.

3. They have six _____.

C Look at the picture. Write.

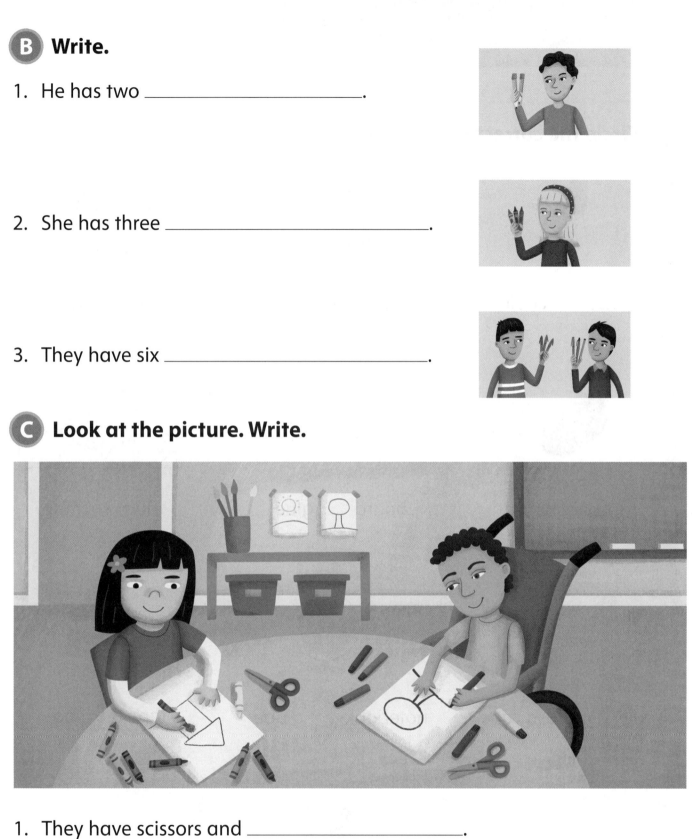

1. They have scissors and _____.

2. She has eight _____.

3. He _____.

The Classroom

A Circle the correct word.

1.

globe　　chair

2.

glue　　notebook

3.

map　　clock

4.

tape　　board

5.

board　　glue

6.

flag　　map

7.

ruler　　trash can

8.

notebook　　globe

9.

tape　　flag

10.

paper　　ruler

11.

trash can　　map

12.

glue　　notebook

1. The paper is _____ the trash can.

2. The map is _____ the board.

3. The globe is _____ the desk.

C **Look at the picture. Write.**

1. The books are on the _____.

2. The map is _____.

3. The paper _____.

A   Match.

magazine   newspaper   atlas   dictionary   DVD

●   ●   ●   ●   ●

●   ●   ●   ●   ●

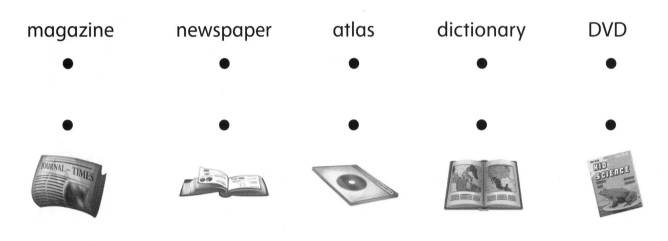

B   Write.

| bookshelves | call number | catalog | return | card |

1. Look in the _____.

2. Go to the _____.

3. Look at the _____.

4. Give the librarian your library _____.

5. Don't forget to _____ the book on time!

C Write.

| checking out | looking | returning |

1. They're _____ a DVD.

2. She's _____ a book.

3. He's _____ at a magazine.

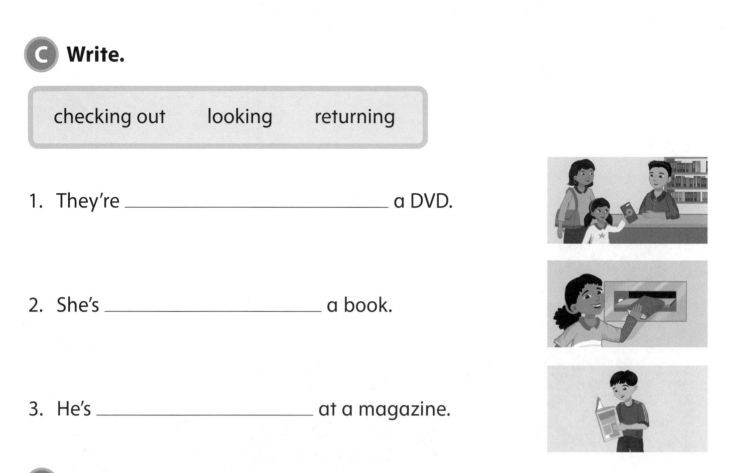

D Look at the picture. Write.

1. He's checking out a _____.

2. She's _____ a DVD.

3. They're _____.

16 The Computer Lab

A Label.

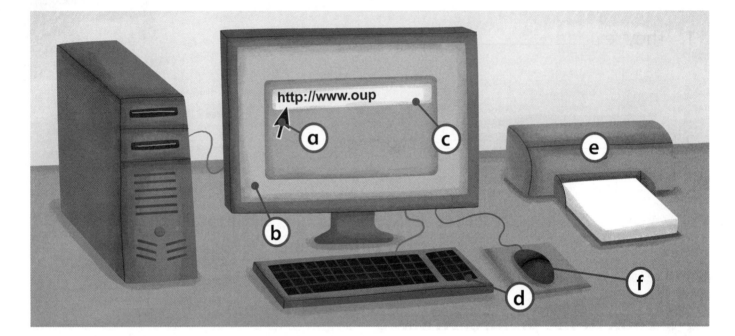

1. _____ printer
2. _____ monitor
3. _____ Internet
4. _____ keyboard
5. _____ mouse
6. _____ cursor

B Write.

click	type	log in

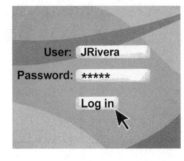

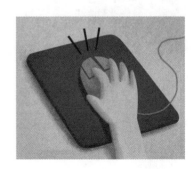

1. _____
2. _____
3. _____

C Write.

headset	computers	microphone

1. She's using a _____.

2. He's using a _____.

3. They're using _____.

D Look at the picture. Write.

1. Felix is using a _____.

2. Sam is _____.

3. Yuko _____.

Lunch in the Cafeteria

A **Match.**

sandwich   juice   strawberries   carrots   crackers   milk

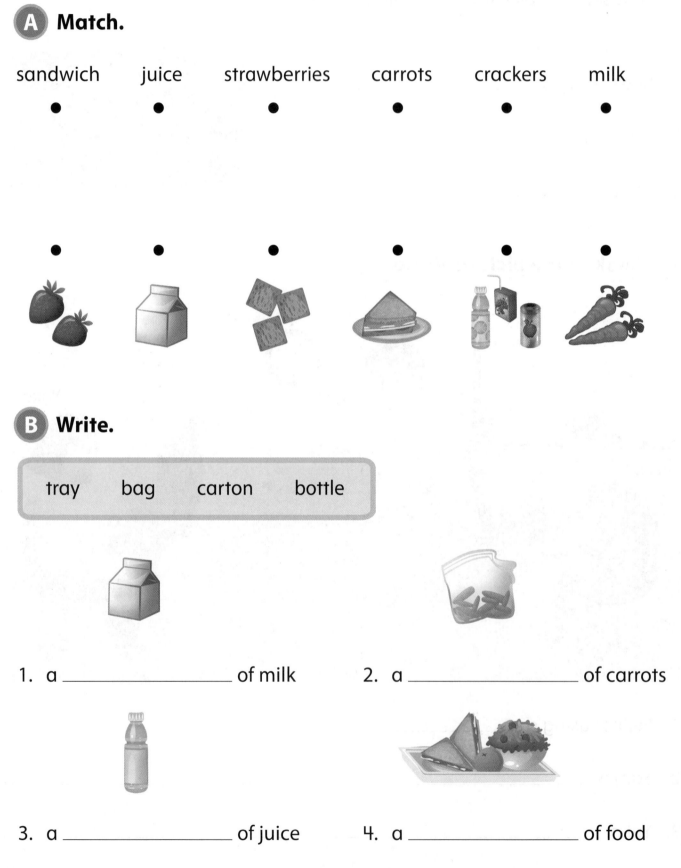

B **Write.**

tray   bag   carton   bottle

1. a _____ of milk

2. a _____ of carrots

3. a _____ of juice

4. a _____ of food

C Write.

1. He has a can of _____.

2. She has a _____ of _____.

3. She has a _____ of _____.

D Look at the picture. Write.

1. Diana has a bottle of juice and a bag of _____.

2. John has a carton of _____.

3. Mia _____.

A Write.

Across

1.
2.
3.
4.
5.
6.

Down

7.
8.
9.
10.
11.
12.

B Write.

catches	kicks	throws

1. He _____ the ball.

2. She _____ the ball.

3. She _____ the ball.

C Look at the picture. Write.

1. Kathy _____ on the court.

2. David _____ on the court.

3. Yaminah _____.

19 The Nurse's Office

A Match.

a.

b.

1. _____ bandage

2. _____ cut

c.

3. _____ fever

4. _____ thermometer

d.

e.

5. _____ sore throat

6. _____ tissues

f.

B Write.

| bleed | lay down | cough | sneeze |

1. _____

2. _____

3. _____

4. _____

C Answer the questions.

> earache fever stomachache

1. What's the matter with Jenny?

   She has a _____.

2. What's the matter with Mark?

   He has an _____.

3. What's the matter with Clara?

   She has a _____.

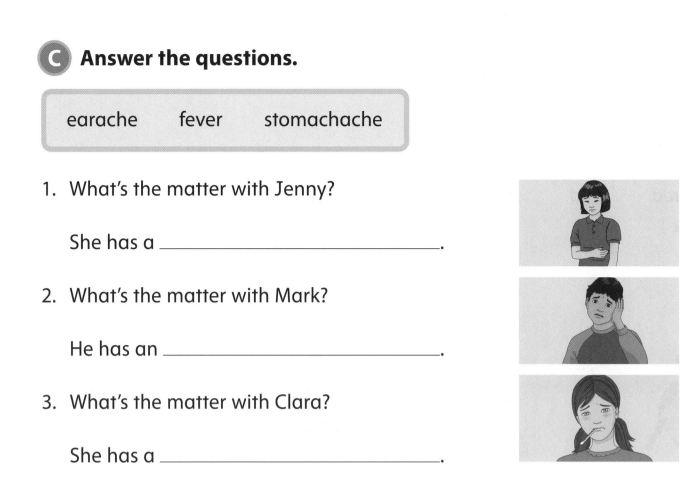

D Look at the picture. Write.

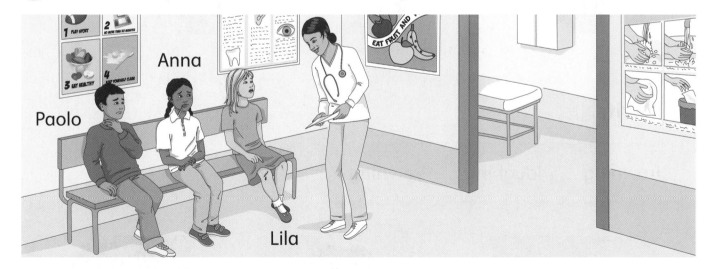

1. Lila has a _____.

2. Anna has _____.

3. Paolo _____.

A Match.

scared   tired   angry   happy   sad   surprised   confused

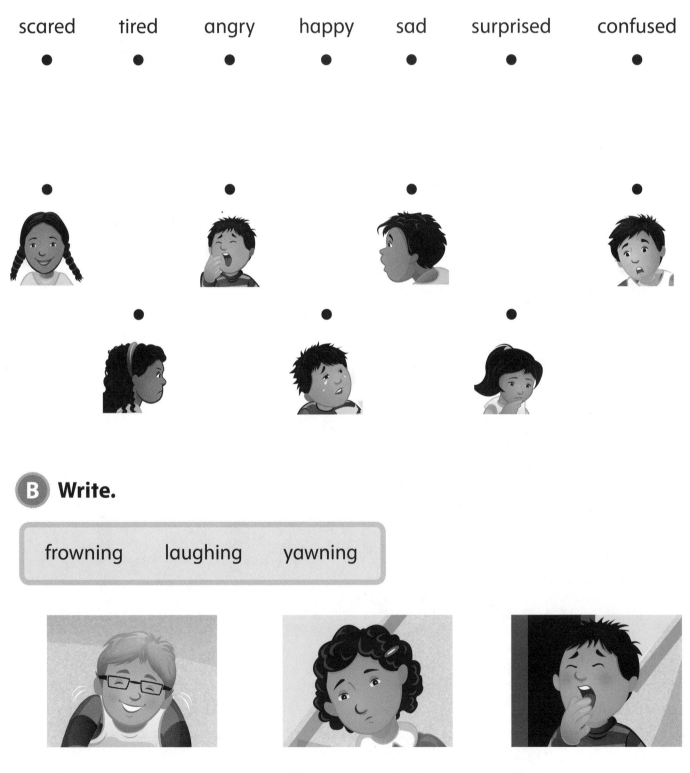

B Write.

| frowning | laughing | yawning |

1. He's _____.
2. She's _____.
3. He's _____.

C Write.

1. He feels _____.

   He's _____.

2. He feels _____.

   He's _____.

3. She feels _____.

   She's _____.

D Look at the picture. Write.

1. The bus driver is _____. He feels _____.

2. The girl is _____. She _____.

3. The boy is _____. _____.

A Label.

| ask | draw | climb | kick | read | run | smile | type |

1. _____

2. _____

3. _____

4. _____

5. _____ questions

6. _____

7. _____

8. _____

B Look at the chart on page 54 of the *Dictionary*. Write.

1. Students read, _____, and draw in the classroom.

2. Students run, _____, and _____ in the gym.

3. Students _____ and _____ in the classroom and the gym.

C Complete the Venn diagram.

bounce   click   jump   laugh   log in   think   throw   write

In the Classroom   In the Gym

_____   _____

_____

_____   _____

_____   _____

_____   _____

D Look at your Venn diagram in C. Write.

1. Students _____ in the classroom and the gym.

2. Students _____ a ball in the _____.

3. Students don't _____ a ball in the _____.

4. Students _____ and _____ in the gym.

5. _____

_____.

A   Match.

1. _____ build houses

2. _____ deliver mail

3. _____ protect the community

4. _____ fix cars

5. _____ sell clothes

6. _____ serve food

7. _____ fight fires

8. _____ grow crops

9. _____ raise animals

10. _____ take care of people

a.

b.

c.

d.

e.

f.

g.

h.

i.

j.

B Write.

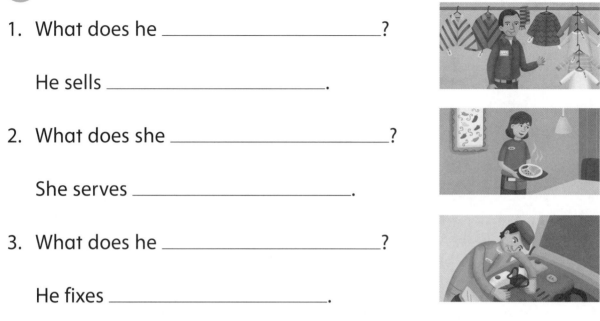

1. What does he _____?

   He sells _____.

2. What does she _____?

   She serves _____.

3. What does he _____?

   He fixes _____.

C Look at the picture. Write.

1. She's a mail carrier. She delivers the _____.

2. He's a police officer. He _____.

3. She's a _____. _____.

A Match.

1. ___ street
2. ___ fence
3. ___ house
4. ___ streetlight
5. ___ address
6. ___ sidewalk
7. ___ street sign
8. ___ apartment building

Look at A. Write *on* or *in*.

1. There's a stop sign _____ the corner.

2. There's a park _____ the street.

3. There's a bench _____ the park.

C **Look at the picture. Write.**

1. There are children in the _____.

2. There's a mother and baby on _____.

3. There's a father and _____.

A Write.

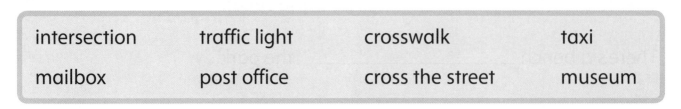

intersection	traffic light	crosswalk	taxi
mailbox	post office	cross the street	museum

1. _____   5. _____

2. _____   6. _____

3. _____   7. _____

4. _____   8. _____

B Look at A. Write.

1. Where is the police officer?

   He's next to the _____.

2. Where is the mail carrier?

   He's next to the _____.

3. Where are the children?

   They're next to the _____.

C Look at the picture. Write.

1. The movie theater is next to the _____.

2. The park is _____.

3. The museum is _____.

A   Where does each person work? Match.

pharmacist   cashier   salesperson   teller

bank   shoe store   drugstore   supermarket

B   Write.

> gas station   supermarket   laundry

1. A customer at the _____ gets clean clothes.

2. A customer at the _____ gets gas.

3. A customer at the _____ gets groceries.

C Write.

| bank | shoe store | supermarket |

1. Where does a teller work?

   A teller works at a _____.

2. Where does a salesperson work?

   A salesperson works at a _____.

3. Where does a cashier work?

   A cashier works at a _____.

D Look at the pictures. Write.

1. The customer is buying bandages at the _____.

2. The customer is buying _____.

3. _____.

A Write.

celery	lettuce	tomato	avocado	apple
pineapple	orange	lemon	paper towels	box

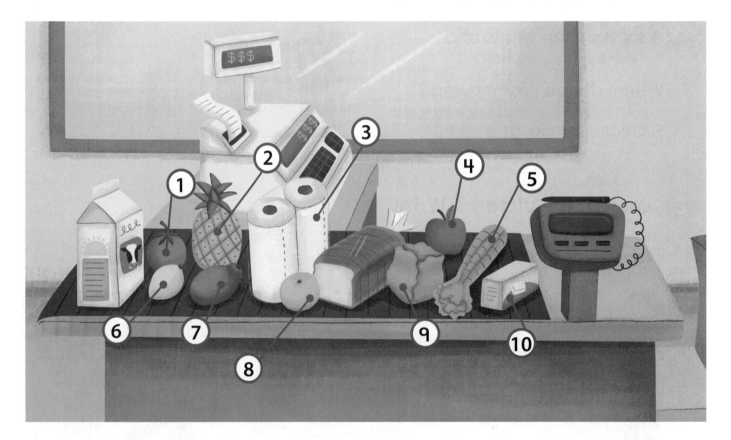

Grocery List

1. _____
2. _____
3. _____
4. _____
5. _____

6. _____
7. _____
8. _____
9. _____
10. _____ of butter

1. She's going to buy an _____.

2. He's going to buy a _____.

3. They're going to buy a _____.

C **Look at the picture. Write.**

1. He's going to buy a carton of _____.

2. She's _____.

3. He's _____.

26   The Restaurant

A Circle the correct word.

1.

   soup   rice

2.

   broccoli   chicken

3.

   chicken   rice

4.

   broccoli   soup

5.

   fork   spoon

6.

   knife   napkin

B Write.

soup   server   order

1. Hello. I'm your

   _____.

2. Can I take your

   _____?

3. I'd like a bowl of

   _____, please.

C Write.

forks	knife	menu

1. She needs a _____.

2. He needs a _____.

3. They need _____.

D Look at the picture. Write.

1. He needs a _____.

2. He needs a _____ and a _____.

3. She _____.

A Label.

helmet   building   bus stop   bicycle   seatbelt   garden

1. _____

2. _____

3. _____

4. _____

5. _____

6. _____

B Write.

Wait   Ride   Walk

1. _____
to the bus stop.

2. _____
for the bus.

3. _____
the bus.

C Write.

rides   walks   drives

1. Sammi _____.

2. Greg _____ a bicycle.

3. Mr. Jones _____ a car.

D Look at the picture. Write.

1. She drives a _____.

2. He _____.

3. She _____.

A Match.

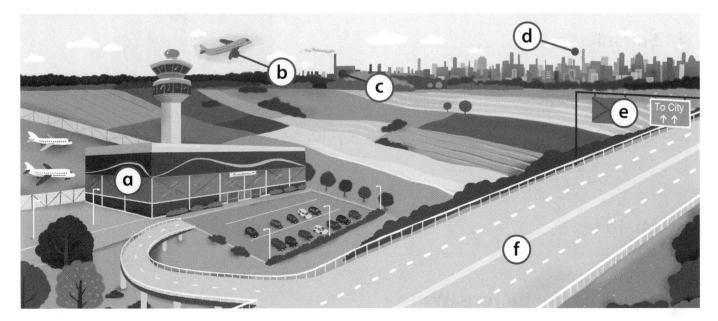

1. ___ airport
2. ___ factory
3. ___ sign
4. ___ skyscraper
5. ___ highway
6. ___ airplane

B Match.

airplane   police car   van   truck   motorcycle   train   helicopter

•   •   •   •   •   •   •

•   •   •   •   •   •   •

C **Look at A. Write *near* or *far*.**

1. The factory is _____ from the airport.

2. The skyscrapers are _____ from the airport.

3. The airport is _____ the highway.

D **Look at the picture. Write.**

1. The van is _____ the airplane.

2. The truck is _____ the airport and

_____ the city.

3. The motorcycle _____.

A Write.

sailboat	crane	tugboat	ferry	dock
lighthouse	ship	life jacket	bridge	

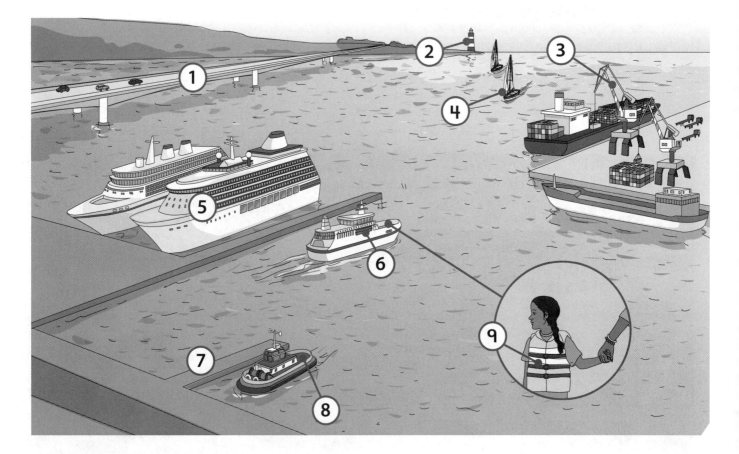

1. _____

2. _____

3. _____

4. _____

5. _____

6. _____

7. _____

8. _____

9. _____

B Look at A. Write.

1. How many lighthouses are on the harbor?

   One _____ is on the harbor.

2. How many _____ are on the bridge?

   Three _____ are on the _____.

3. How many _____ are in the harbor?

   Eight _____ are in the _____.

C Look at the picture. Write.

1. Ten people are on the _____.

2. Four people are _____.

3. Two _____.

A Match.

1. _____ cast

2. _____ X-ray

3. _____ wheelchair

4. _____ shot

5. _____ ambulance

6. _____ crutches

a.

b.

c.

d.

e.

f.

B Match.

1.

2.

3.

surgeon

patient

receptionist

paramedic

doctor

baby

4.

5.

6.

C Write.

1. Who is in the ambulance?

   The _____ is in the ambulance.

2. Who is in the emergency room?

   The _____ is in the emergency room.

3. Who is in the wheelchair?

   The _____ is in the wheelchair.

D Look at the pictures. Write.

  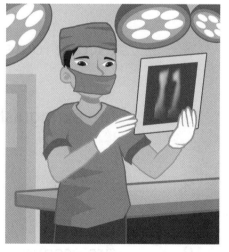

1. The _____ is in the nursery.

2. The _____ the emergency room.

3. _____.

31 Fire Safety

A Match.

1. _____ firefighter

2. _____ smoke

3. _____ fire truck

4. _____ matches

5. _____ uniform

6. _____ smoke detector

7. _____ escape route

8. _____ fire extinguisher

9. _____ battery

10. _____ fire escape

11. _____ exit

12. _____ call 911

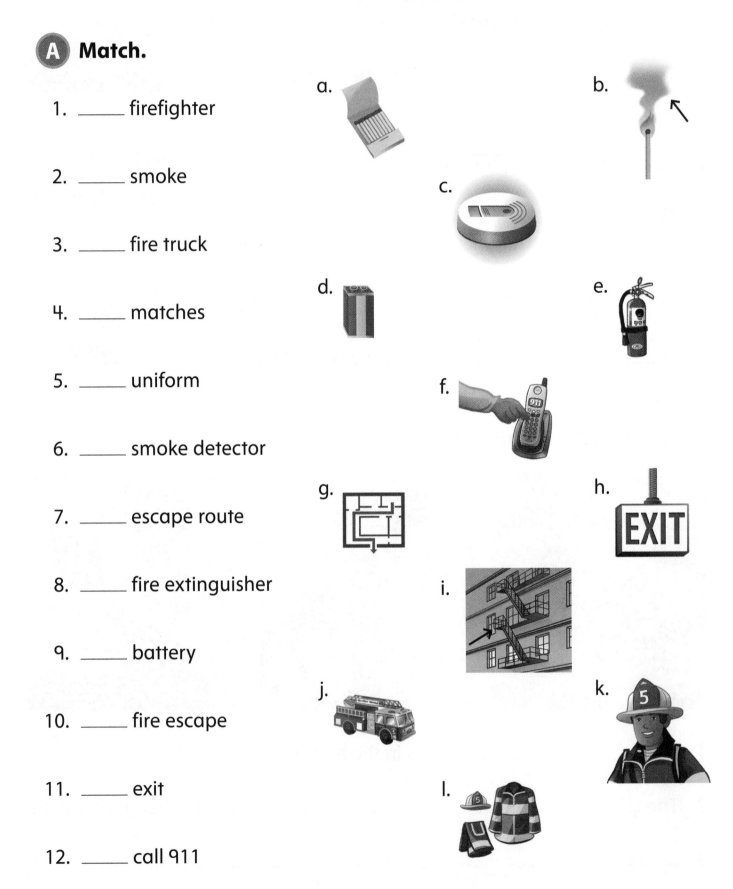

a.

b.

c.

d.

e.

f.

g.

h. EXIT

i.

j.

k.

l.

B Write.

smoke detector   911   matches

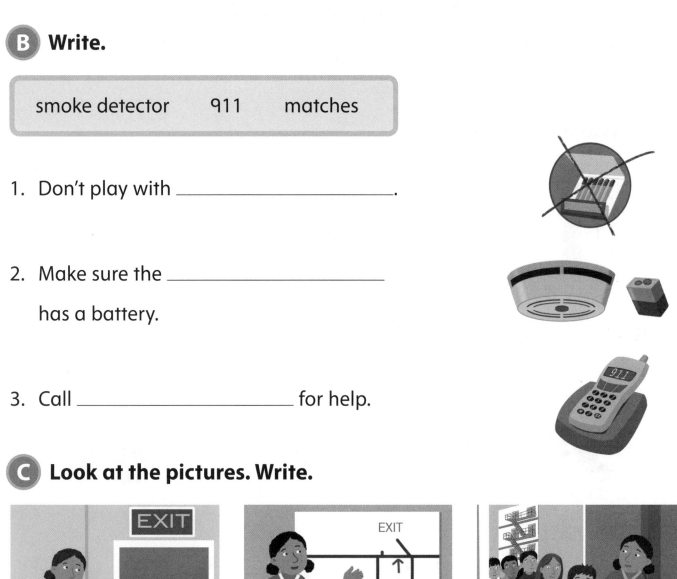

1. Don't play with _____.

2. Make sure the _____

   has a battery.

3. Call _____ for help.

C Look at the pictures. Write.

1. Know the _____.

2. Plan an _____.

3. Find the _____.

A Circle the correct word.

1. farmer horse

2. tractor barn

3. cow chicken

4. horse cow

5. horse farmer

6. chicken tractor

B Label.

crop orchard field

1. _____

2. _____

3. _____

C Write.

pick	feeds	plows

1. The farmer _____ the field.

2. She _____ the cow.

3. They _____ apples in the orchard.

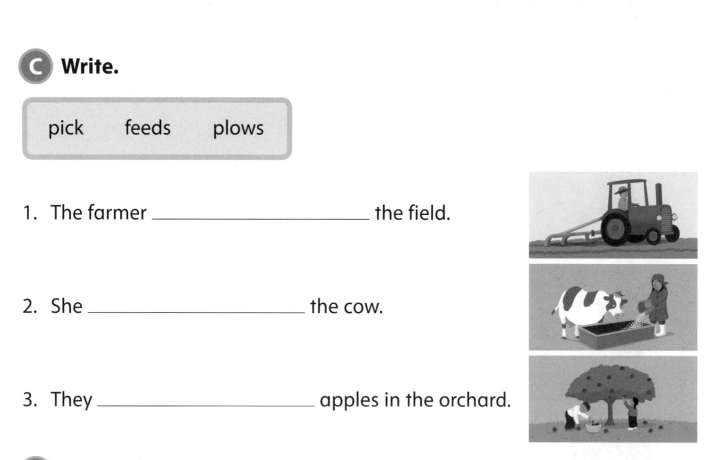

D Look at the picture. Write.

1. She picks _____.

2. He plows _____.

3. They _____.

A Match.

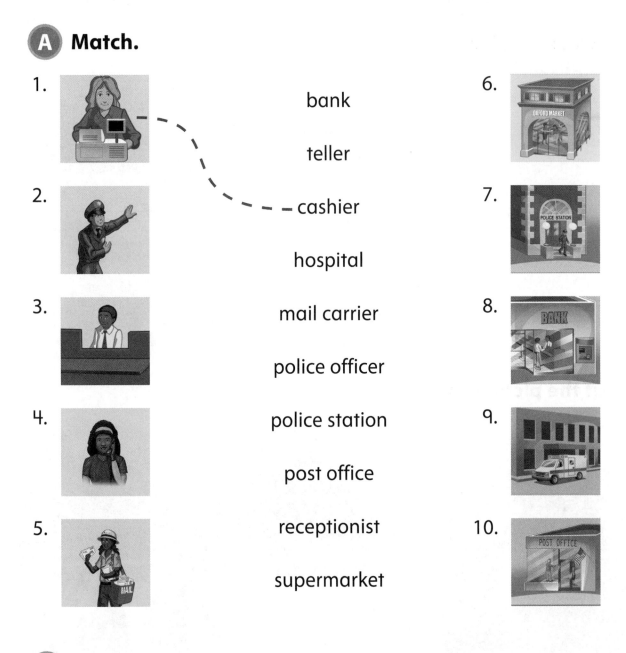

1.

bank

teller

2.   cashier   7.

hospital

3.   mail carrier   8.

police officer

4.   police station   9.

post office

5.   receptionist   10.

supermarket

B Look at the chart on page 80 of the *Dictionary*. Write.

1. A _____ works at a supermarket.

2. A police officer works at a _____.

3. A _____ works at a bank.

4. A _____ works at a post office.

C Complete the chart.

doctor	drugstore	farmer	farm	hospital
pharmacist	restaurant	salesperson	server	shoe store

People Who Work ⟶	**Places to Work**

D Look at your chart in C. Write.

1. A server works at a _____.

2. A _____ works at a hospital.

3. A _____ works at a _____.

4. _____.

5. _____.

A Label.

trade	explore	invent	travel	sign a document
celebrate	be born	die	immigrate	

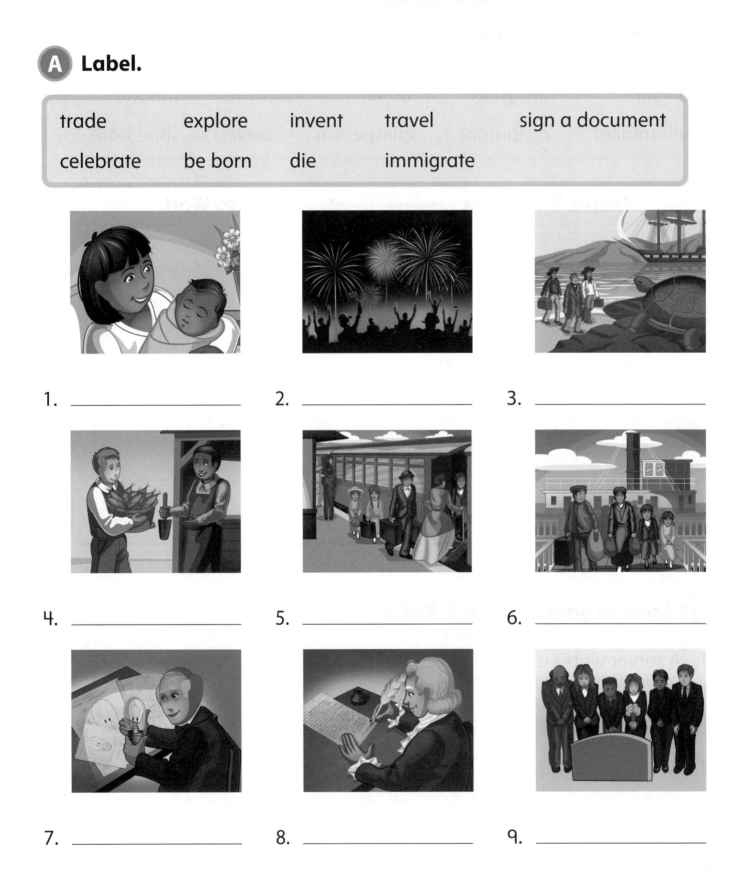

1. _____

2. _____

3. _____

4. _____

5. _____

6. _____

7. _____

8. _____

9. _____

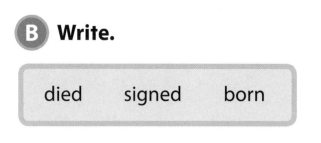

B **Write.**

| died | signed | born |

1. George Washington was _____ in 1732.

2. He _____ the Constitution in 1787.

3. He _____ in 1799.

C **Look at the pictures. Write.**

2002   2009   2010

1. Marco was _____ in _____.

2. He _____ to Washington, D.C. in _____.

3. He _____ his eighth birthday in _____.

Match.

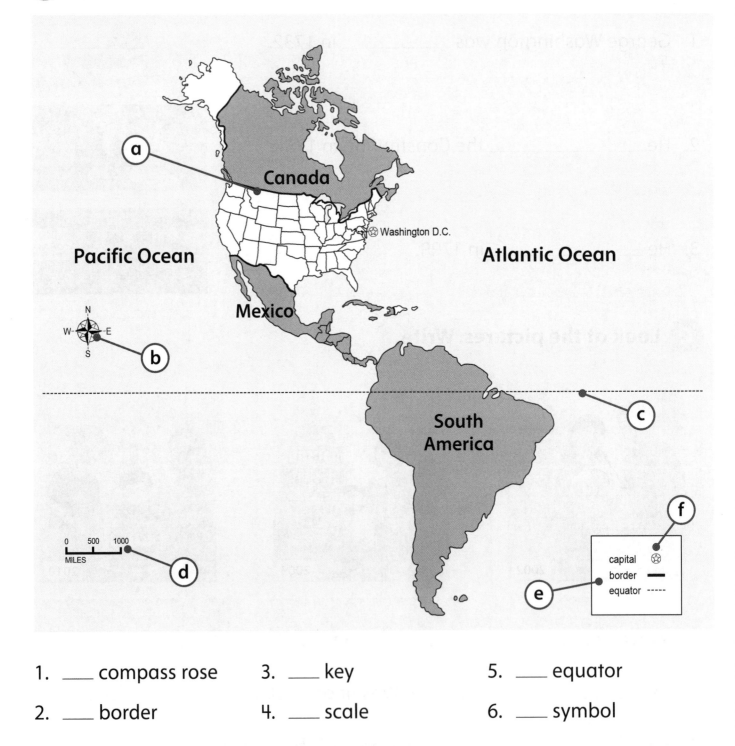

1. ___ compass rose
2. ___ border
3. ___ key
4. ___ scale
5. ___ equator
6. ___ symbol

B Write.

1. This is a _____.

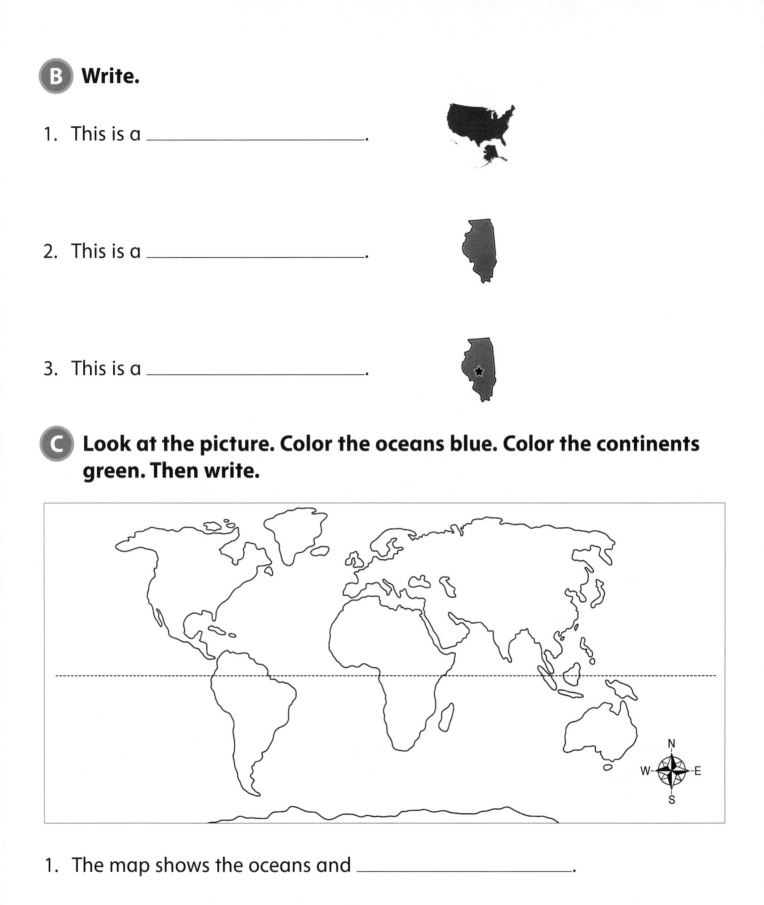

2. This is a _____.

3. This is a _____.

C Look at the picture. Color the oceans blue. Color the continents green. Then write.

1. The map shows the oceans and _____.

2. The color blue shows _____.

3. The color green _____.

A Write.

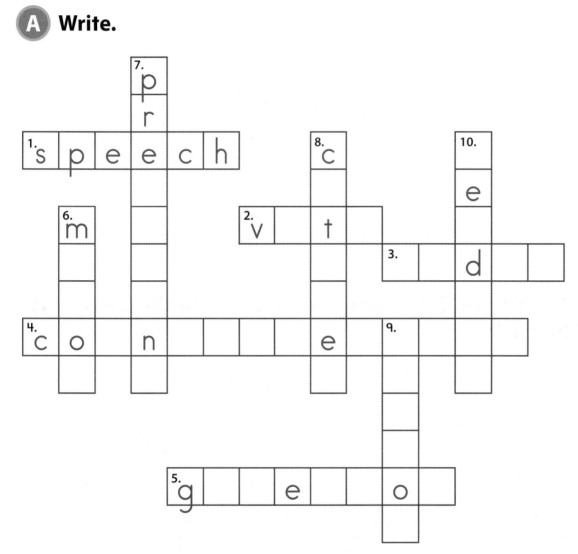

Across

1.
2.
3.
4.
5.

Down

6.
7.
8.
9.
10.

Write.

president	judge	city council

1. Who leads the citizens?

   The _____ leads the citizens.

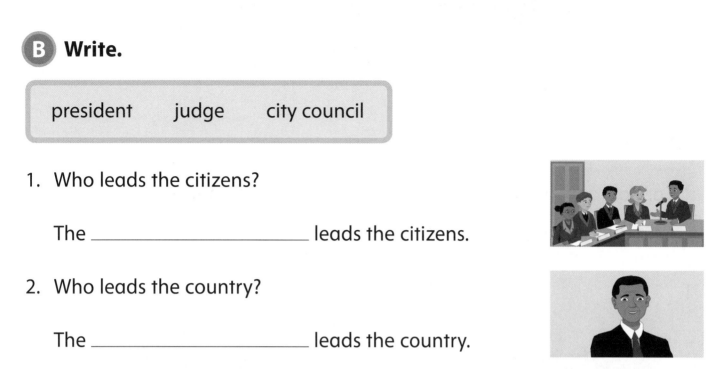

2. Who leads the country?

   The _____ leads the country.

3. Who leads the courtroom?

   The _____ leads the courtroom.

Look at the pictures. Write.

1. The mayor leads the _____.

2. The governor _____.

3. _____.

A Label.

Capitol	Congress	Supreme Court	monument
memorial	stars	stripes	Pledge of Allegiance

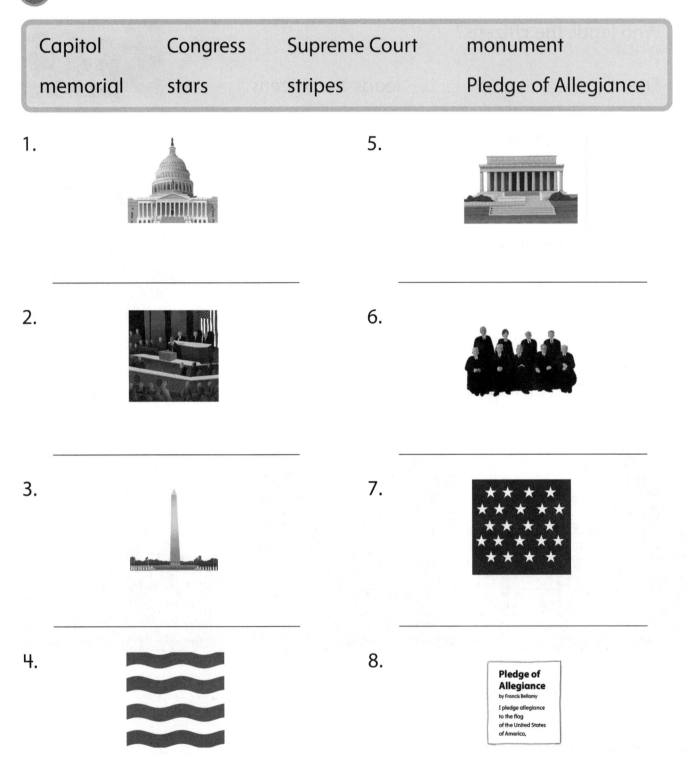

1.

_____

2.

_____

3.

_____

4.

_____

5.

_____

6.

_____

7.

_____

8.

_____

B Write.

national anthem	White House	eagle

1. What is the bald _____?

   It's a national symbol.

2. What is "The Star Spangled Banner"?

   It's the _____.

3. What is the _____?

   It's the home of the President.

C Look at the pictures. Write.

1. The Lincoln Memorial is a national _____.

2. The Statue of Liberty is a _____.

3. The Capitol is a _____.

A   Match.

1. _____ monument

a.

b.

2. _____ Supreme Court

c.

The Star Spangled Banner
by Francis Scott Key
September 14th, 1814

O! say can you see
by the dawn's early light,

3. _____ city council

4. _____ governor

d.

e.

5. _____ national anthem

B   Look at the chart on page 90 in the *Dictionary*. Write.

1. The city has a _____ and

   a _____.

2. The state has a _____ and a _____.

3. The country has a _____, a _____,

   and a _____.

C **Complete the chart.**

The United States			
	country	state	city
Congress			
mayor			
citizens			
president			
memorial			

D **Look at your chart in C. Write.**

1. The country has a president, Congress, and _____.

2. The country doesn't have a _____.

3. The state has a _____ and _____.

4. The state doesn't have a _____.

5. _____.

37 Healthy Habits

A Match.

exercise   sleep   floss   drink water   wear sunblock

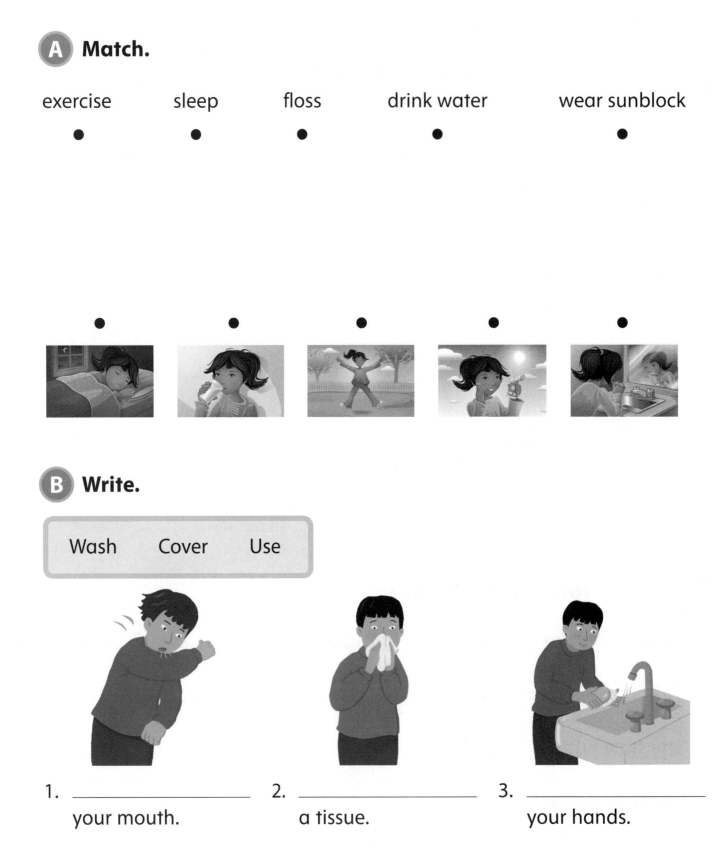

B Write.

Wash	Cover	Use

1. _____
your mouth.

2. _____
a tissue.

3. _____
your hands.

C Write.

goes to the dentist   gets a checkup   exercises

1. She _____ every day.

2. He _____ every six months.

3. She _____ every year.

D Look at the pictures. Write.

1. She _____ every day.

2. He _____.

3. She _____.

A Write.

cheek	eyebrow	tongue	chin	teeth	ear
mouth	lip	eyelid	gum	nose	forehead

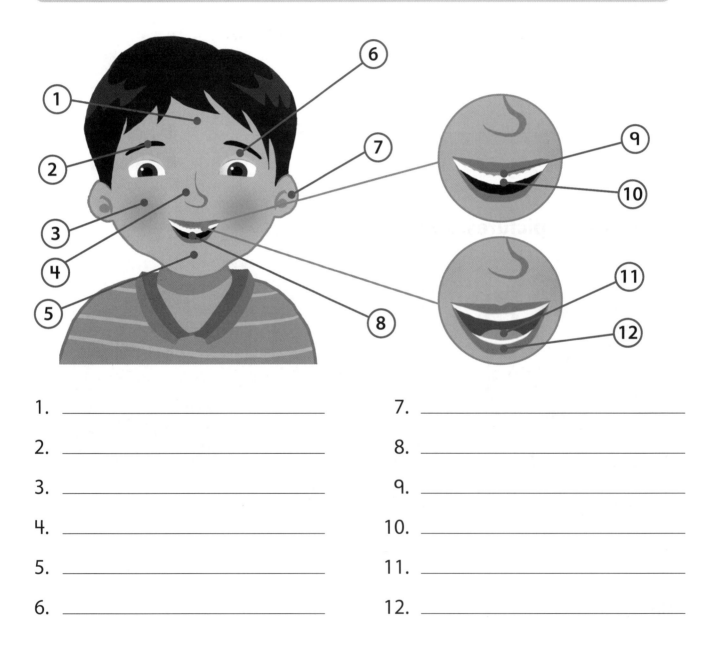

1. _____   7. _____

2. _____   8. _____

3. _____   9. _____

4. _____   10. _____

5. _____   11. _____

6. _____   12. _____

B Look at A. Write *above* or *below.*

1. His forehead is _____ his eyebrows.

2. His eyebrows are _____ his eyelids.

3. His cheeks are _____ his eyes.

C Look at the picture. Write.

Lucy   Tasha   Emma

1. Lucy's eyes and nose are _____.

2. Tasha's nose and _____.

3. Emma's lips and _____.

A Write the missing vowels: *a, e, i, o,* or *u.*

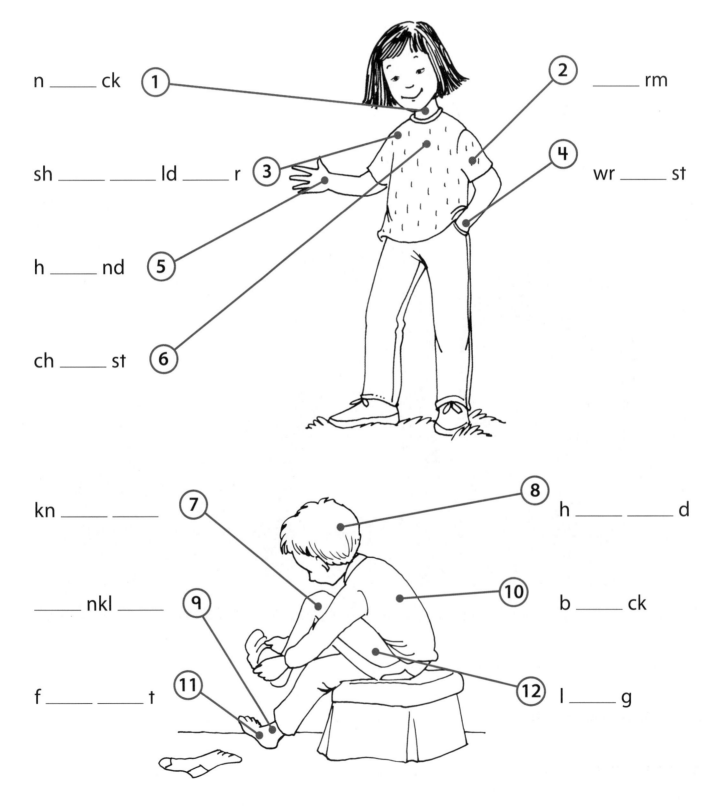

n _____ ck ①

② _____ rm

sh _____ _____ ld _____ r ③

④ wr _____ st

h _____ nd ⑤

ch _____ st ⑥

kn _____ _____ _____ ⑦

⑧ h _____ _____ d

_____ nkl _____ ⑨

⑩ b _____ ck

f _____ _____ t ⑪

⑫ l _____ g

B Write.

shoulders   foot   head   hand   leg   arm

1. The ankle is between the _____

   and the _____.

2. The wrist is between the _____

   and the _____.

3. The neck is between the _____

   and the _____.

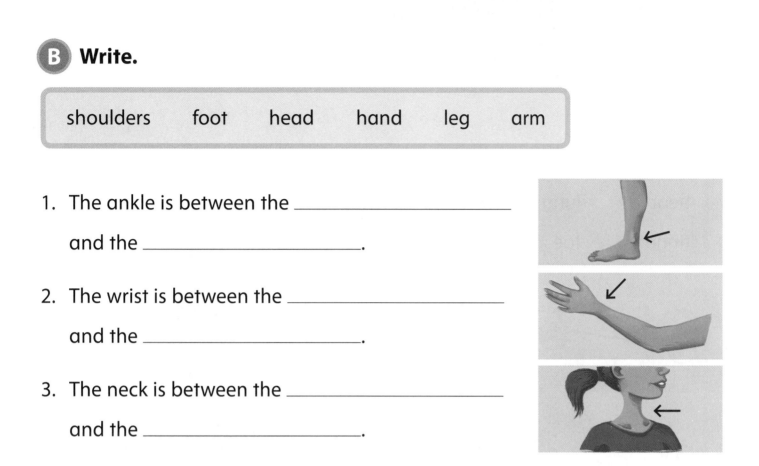

C Look at the picture. Write.

1. The chest is between the _____ and the arms.

2. The ankle _____.

3. The wrist _____.

A Write.

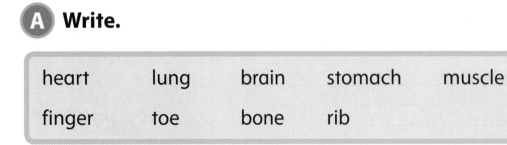

| heart | lung | brain | stomach | muscle |
| finger | toe | bone | rib | |

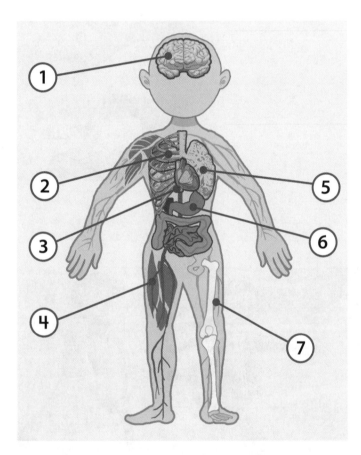

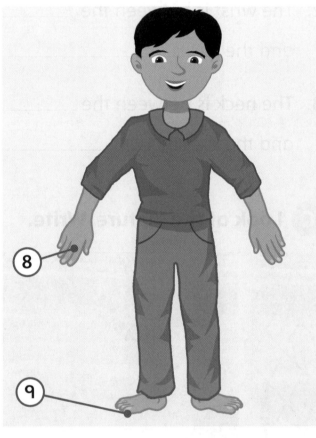

1. _____

2. _____

3. _____

4. _____

5. _____

6. _____

7. _____

8. _____

9. _____

1. The _____ is in the head.

2. The _____ is in the chest.

3. The _____ is on the body.

C Look at the picture. Write.

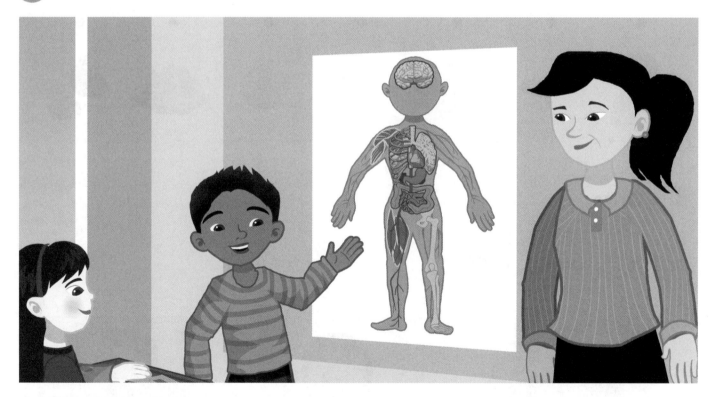

1. The lungs and heart are in the _____.

2. The brain is _____.

3. The muscles and bones _____.

A Match.

shiny   rough   smooth   sweet   sour   loud   quiet

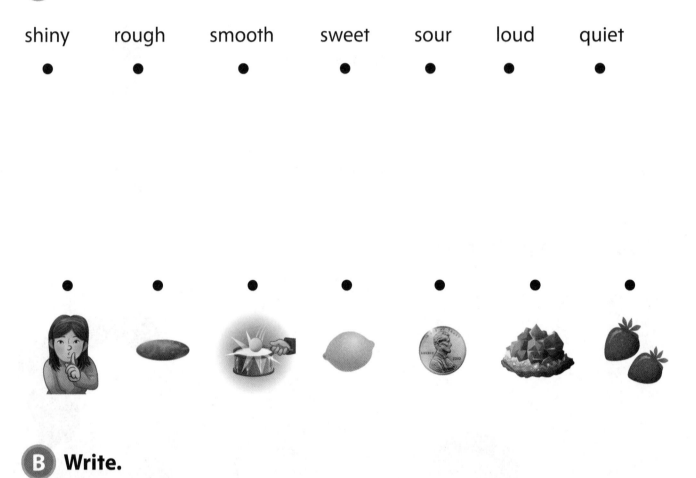

B Write.

Feel   See   Hear

1. _____
the shiny airplane.

2. _____
the loud music.

3. _____
the smooth stone.

C Write.

| sees | tastes | smells |

1. He _____ the sour lemon.

2. She _____ the sweet flower.

3. He _____ the shiny star.

D Look at the picture. Write.

What is it? Use your senses to find out.

1. He hears the _____ triangle.

2. He feels the _____.

3. He _____.

A Match.

1. _____ nuts

2. _____ peach

3. _____ corn

4. _____ pear

5. _____ oatmeal

6. _____ peppers

7. _____ pasta

8. _____ fish

9. _____ cheese

10. _____ sweet potato

11. _____ yogurt

12. _____ spinach

a.

b.

c.

d.

e.

f.

g.

h.

i.

j.

k.

l.

B Write.

1. _____ are part of the

   meat and bean group.

2. _____ and

   _____ are part of the

   milk group.

3. _____ and

   _____ are part of the

   vegetable group.

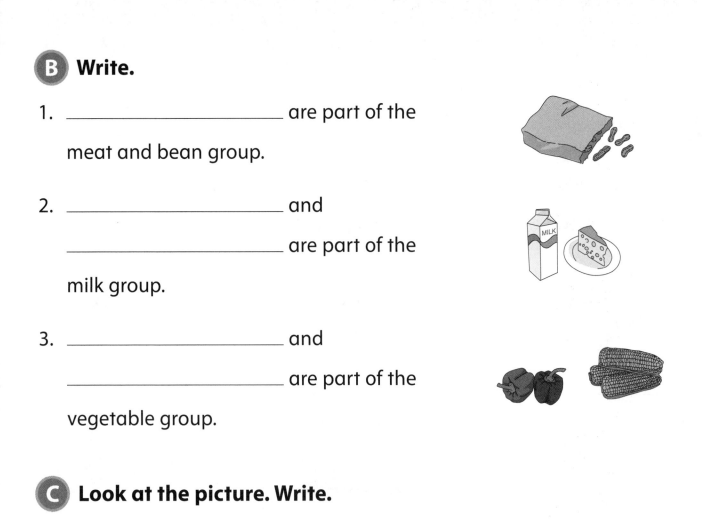

C Look at the picture. Write.

1. Sweet potatoes and spinach are part of the _____.

2. Peaches and _____.

3. Bread _____.

A Label.

bone	heart	lips	lungs	neck
toe	head	eyebrow	fingernail	

1. _____

2. _____

3. _____

4. _____

5. _____

6. _____

7. _____

8. _____

9. _____

B Look at the chart on page 104 of the *Dictionary*. Write.

1. I have many toes, _____, and _____.

2. I have two eyebrows, _____,
   and _____.

3. I have one head, _____, and _____.

Complete the chart.

| back | brain | ears | knees | muscles |
| shoulders | stomach | teeth | toenails | |

Parts of the Body		
one	**two**	**many**

D **Look at your chart in C. Write.**

1. I have _____ stomach.

2. I have _____ knees.

3. I have _____ teeth and muscles.

4. I don't have two _____.

5. I don't have _____.

6. _____.

105

A Label.

ruler	magnifying glass	measure	thermometer	binoculars
observe	measuring cup	microscope	measuring tape	meter stick

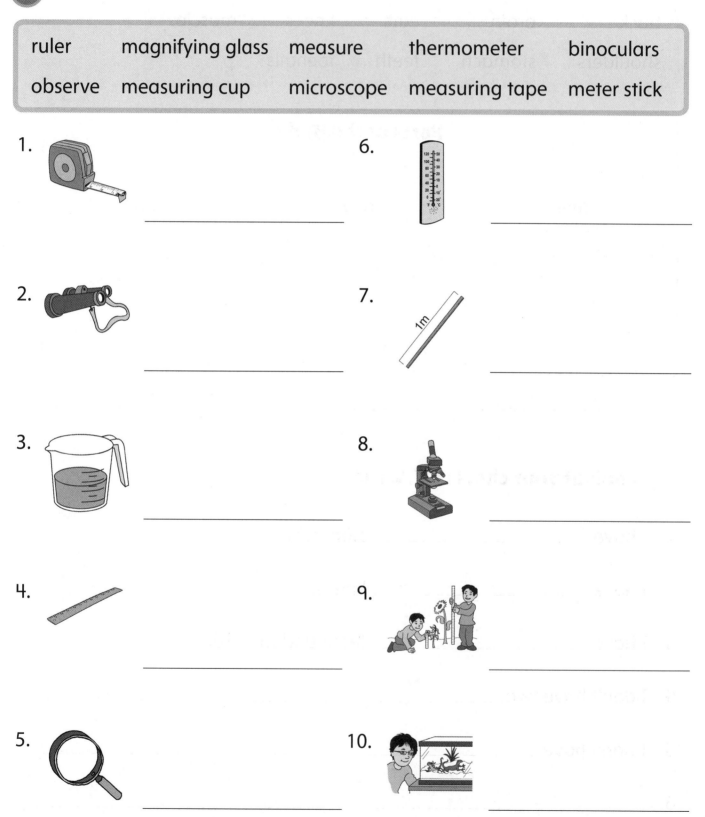

1. _____

2. _____

3. _____

4. _____

5. _____

6. _____

7. _____

8. _____

9. _____

10. _____

B **Write *measure* or *observe*.**

1. Use a microscope to

   _____.

2. Use a thermometer to

   _____.

3. Use binoculars to

   _____.

C **Look at the picture. Write.**

1. Use a measuring tape to _____.

2. Use a _____ to observe.

3. Use a _____.

A Write.

thorn	petal	bulb	pollen	bee	flower
seed	seedling	stem	roots	bud	leaf

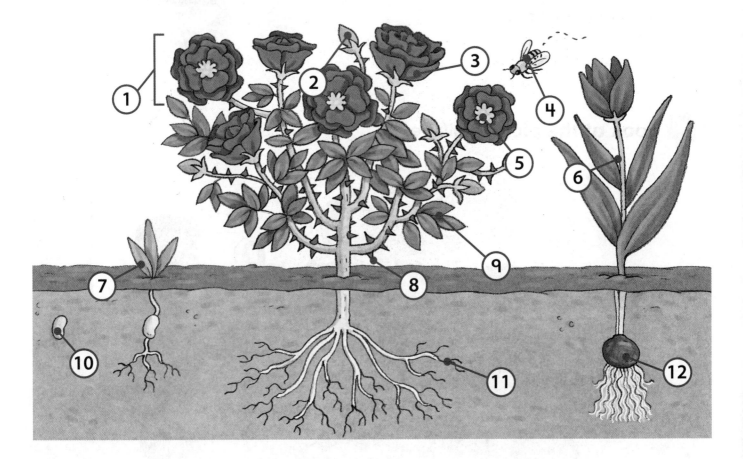

1. _____

2. _____

3. _____

4. _____

5. _____

6. _____

7. _____

8. _____

9. _____

10. _____

11. _____

12. _____

B **Write *large* or *small*.**

1. The beans have _____ seeds.

2. The seedling has _____ leaves.

3. The rose has _____ thorns.

C **Look at the picture. Write.**

1. Sunflowers have large flowers and _____ seeds.

2. Tulips have _____ leaves and

   _____ petals.

3. Roses _____.

A Label.

tail	beak	wing	feather	paw	fur
claw	hoof	antlers	pouch	whiskers	shell

1. _____

2. _____

3. _____

4. _____

5. _____

6. _____

7. _____

8. _____

9. _____

10. _____

11. _____

12. _____

Write.

1. Which animal has fur?

   The _____ has fur.

2. Which animal has feathers?

   The _____ has feathers.

3. Which animals have tails?

   The _____ and the _____ have tails.

C **Look at the picture. Write.**

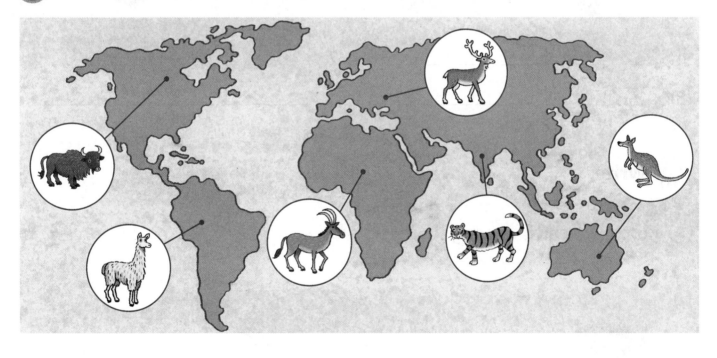

1. The kangaroo has a _____ and a _____.

2. The antelope has _____ and _____.

3. The tiger, the antelope, and the kangaroo have _____.

111

A **Write.**

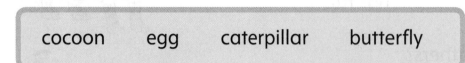
cocoon   egg   caterpillar   butterfly

1. _____   2. _____

3. _____   4. _____

B **Write.**

hatch   chick   egg   nest

1.

_____

2.

_____

3.

_____

4.

_____

C Write.

cat   tadpole   bird   kitten   frog   chick

1. The _____

   becomes a _____ .

2. The _____

   becomes a _____ .

3. The _____

   becomes a _____ .

D Look at the picture. Write.

1. The chicks become _____ .

2. The caterpillar becomes a _____ .

3. _____ .

A **Write the words in the puzzle.**

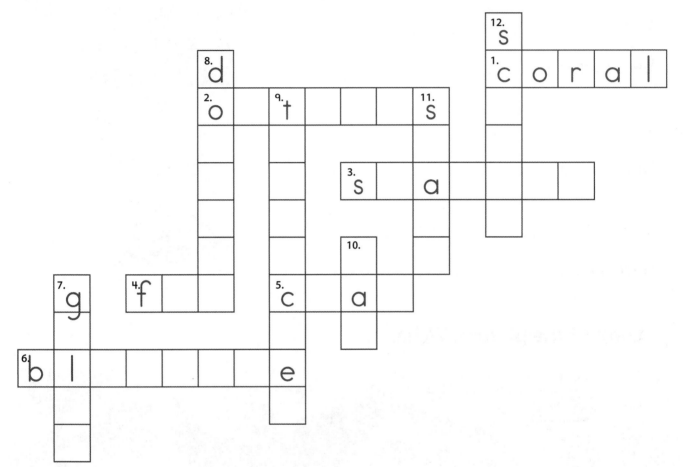

Across

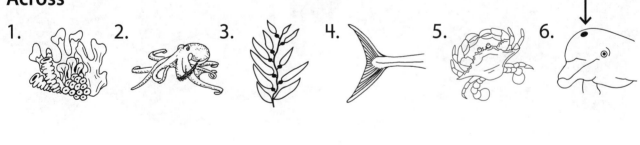

Down

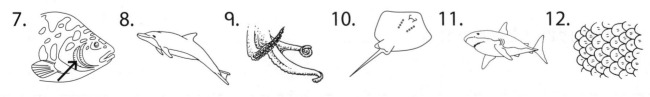

Write.

1. A _____

   has _____ .

2. An _____

   has _____ .

3. A _____

   has a _____ .

C **Look at the picture. Write.**

1. A crab has claws and a _____ .

2. An octopus has eight _____ and

   a crab has eight _____ .

3. A shark and a ray have _____ .

115

A Match.

1. _____ coyote

2. _____ hawk

3. _____ lizard

4. _____ mouse

5. _____ prairie dog

6. _____ rabbit

7. _____ scorpion

8. _____ snake

a.
b.
c.
d.
e.
f.
g.
h.

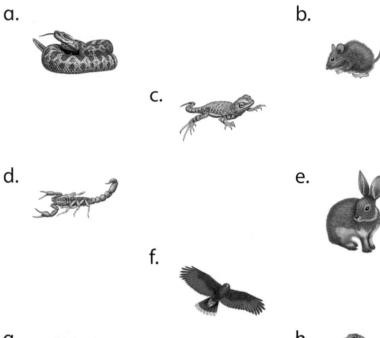

B Write.

| dunes | hole | cactus | sand |

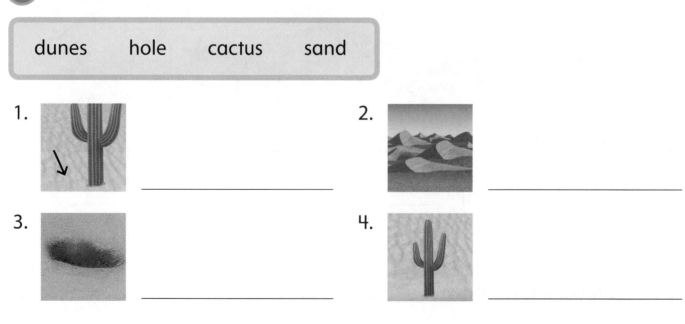

1. _____

2. _____

3. _____

4. _____

C Write.

1. The _____ hides under the rock.

2. The _____ hides in the hole.

3. The _____ hides

   in the _____.

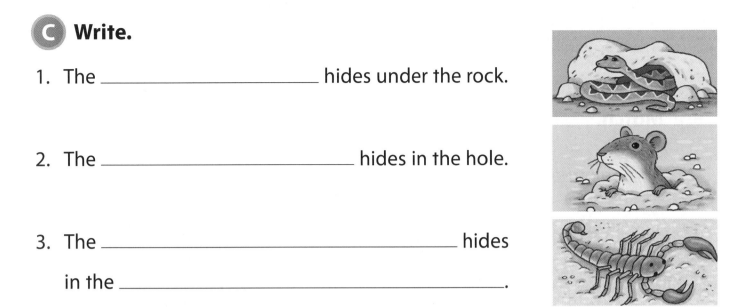

D Look at the picture. Write.

1. The bird hides in the _____.

2. The lizard _____.

3. _____.

49 The Forest

A Match.

1. _____ oak tree

2. _____ needles

3. _____ acorns

4. _____ pine tree

5. _____ pine cone

a

b

c

d

e

B Write.

| deer | mosquito | squirrel | woodpecker | bear |

1.

_____

2.

_____

3.

_____

4.

_____

5.

_____

C Write.

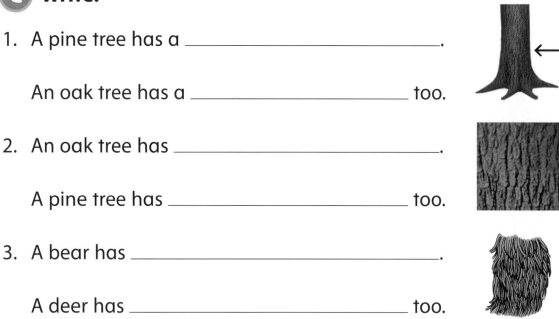

1. A pine tree has a _____.

   An oak tree has a _____ too.

2. An oak tree has _____.

   A pine tree has _____ too.

3. A bear has _____.

   A deer has _____ too.

D Look at the picture. Write.

1. An oak tree and a pine tree have _____.

2. A hawk and a woodpecker _____.

3. A rabbit and _____.

50 The Rain Forest

A Match.

1. 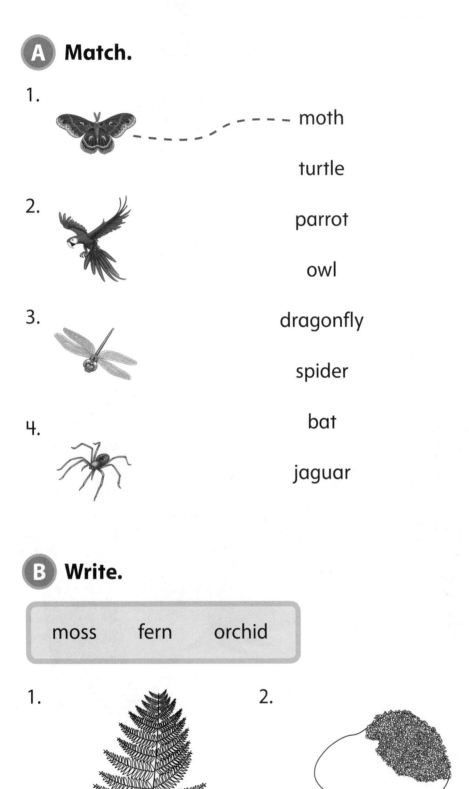 - - - - - moth

   turtle

2. parrot

   owl

3. dragonfly

   spider

4. bat

   jaguar

5.

6.

7.

8.

B Write.

| moss | fern | orchid |

1.

2.

3.

_____   _____   _____

C **Write *flies* or *walks*.**

1. A bat _____.

2. An owl _____.

3. An ant _____.

D **Look at the picture. Write.**

1. An ant and a spider _____.

2. A _____ and a _____ fly.

3. A jaguar and _____.

A **Write.**

elephant	hyena	lion	flamingo
hippopotamus	giraffe	zebra	leopard

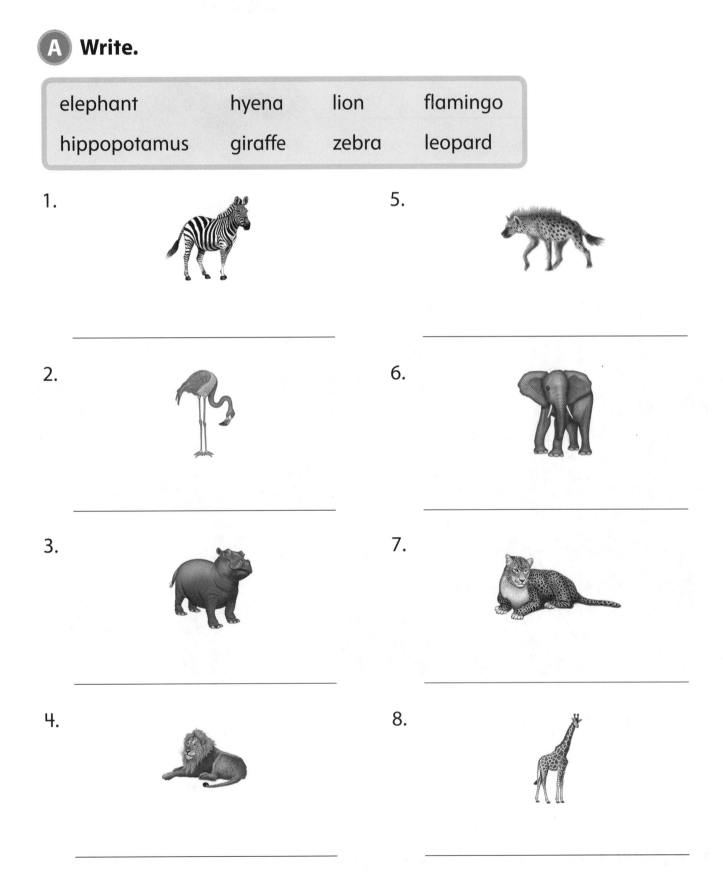

1.

_____

2.

_____

3.

_____

4.

_____

5.

_____

6.

_____

7.

_____

8.

_____

B **Write *spots* or *stripes*.**

1. A leopard has _____.

2. A zebra has _____.

3. A giraffe has _____.

C **Look at the picture. Write.**

1. The elephants are near the _____.

2. The zebras are far from _____.

3. The lion _____.

A Label.

| fin | tail | paw | wing |

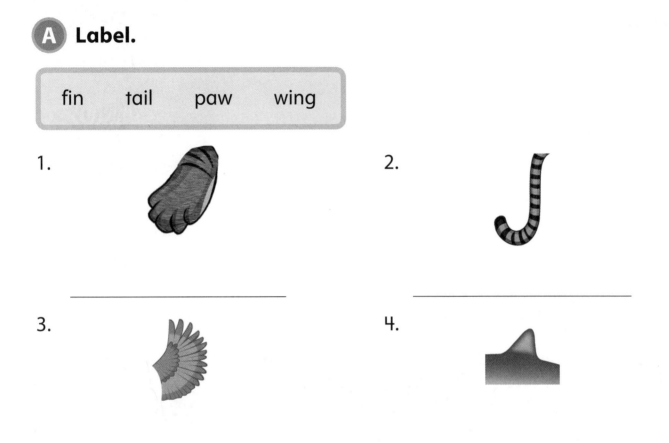

1. _____

2. _____

3. _____

4. _____

B   Look at the chart on page 124 of the *Dictionary.* Write.

1. A _____ has a tail and fins.

2. A _____ has a tail and wings.

3. A _____ and a _____ have a tail and paws.

4. A fish, squirrel, lion, _____, and _____ have a tail.

C **Complete the chart.**

Animal Features		feathers	scales	fur
fish				
snake				
squirrel				
parrot				
lion				

D **Look at your chart in C. Write.**

1. A parrot has _____.

2. A parrot does not have _____ or _____.

3. A squirrel and a lion have _____.

4. A squirrel and a lion do not have _____.

5. _____.

A Match.

1. _____ predict

2. _____ test

3. _____ pour

4. _____ record

5. _____ compare

6. _____ sort

7. _____ explain

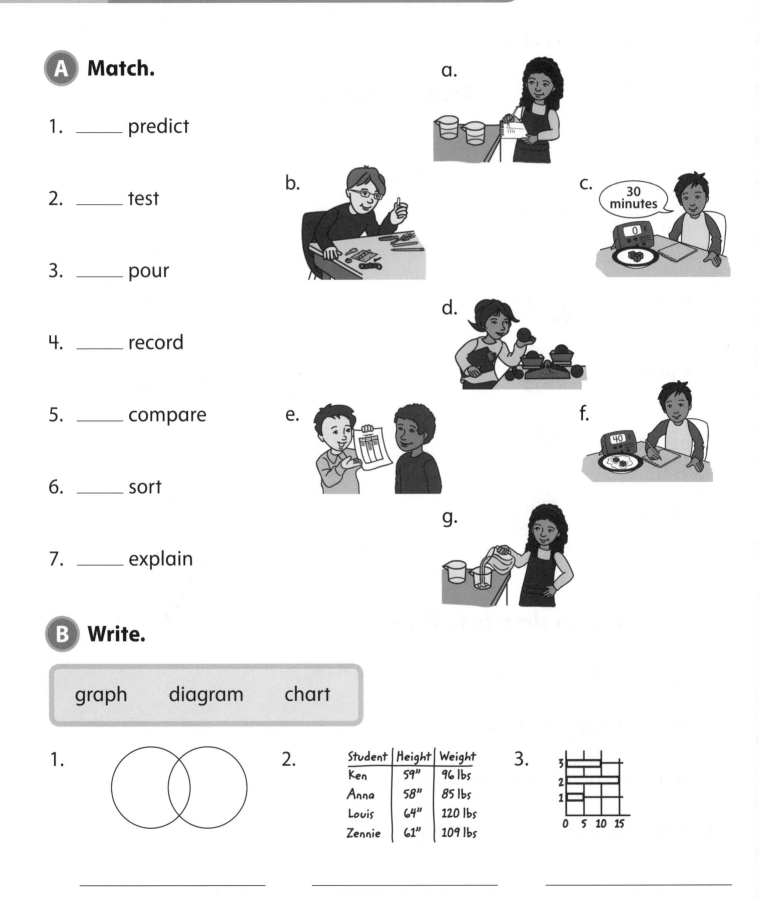

a.

b.

c. 30 minutes

d.

e.

f.

g.

B Write.

| graph | diagram | chart |

1.

2.

Student	Height	Weight
Ken	59"	96 lbs
Anna	58"	85 lbs
Louis	64"	120 lbs
Zennie	61"	109 lbs

3.

_____   _____   _____

C Write.

1. First, _____.

   Then, _____ it.

2. First, _____.

   Then, _____ a diagram.

3. First, make a _____.

   Then, _____ it.

D Look at the pictures. Write.

1. _____, predict. _____, test it.

2. First, _____ the milk and the water.

   Then, _____ the weights.

3. _____.

A Match.

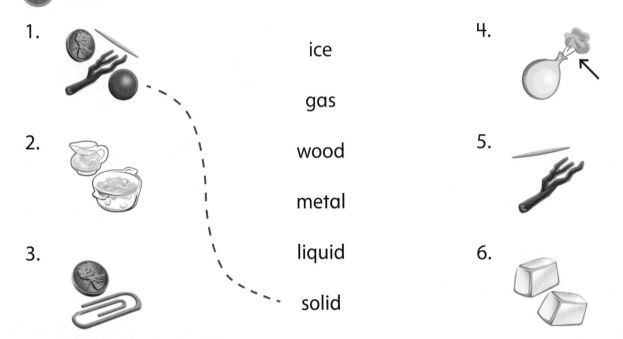

1.

2.

3.

ice

gas

wood

metal

liquid

solid

4.

5.

6.

B Write.

| freeze | mix | boil | float | sink | melt |

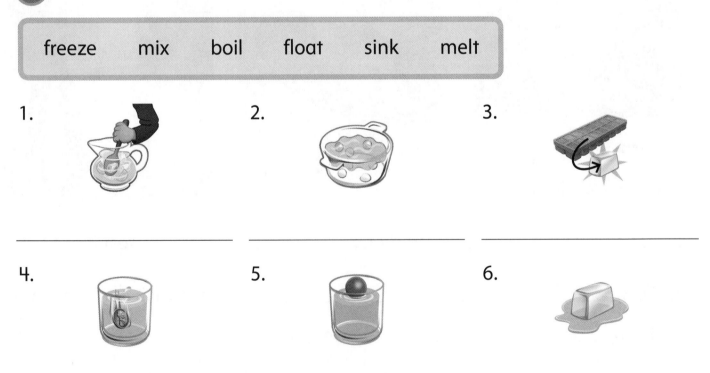

1.

2.

3.

4.

5.

6.

C Write *float, sink,* or *melt.*

1. Does metal _____?

   Yes, metal _____s.

2. Does wood _____?

   Yes, wood _____s.

3. Does ice _____?

   Yes, ice _____s.

D Look at the pictures. Write.

1. She _____ the water to make _____ cubes.

2. She _____ the _____ to make tea.

3. He _____ the _____,

   _____, and lemon to make iced tea.

A Write the words in the puzzle.

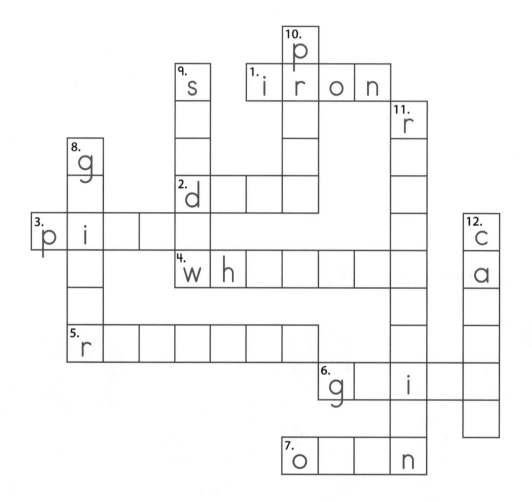

Across

1.
2.
3.
4.
5.
6.
7.

Down

8.
9.
10.
11.
12.

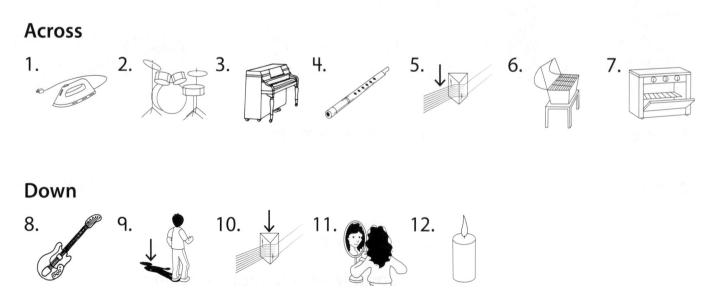

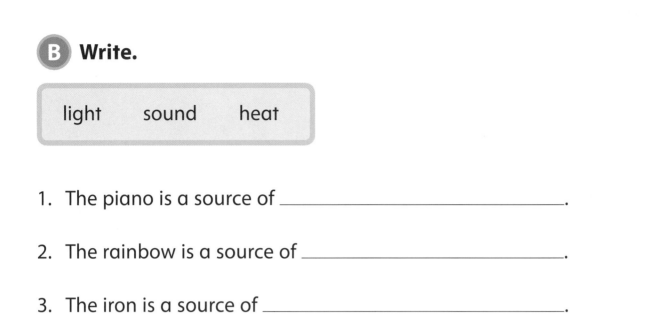

B Write.

| light | sound | heat |

1. The piano is a source of _____.

2. The rainbow is a source of _____.

3. The iron is a source of _____.

C Look at the picture. Write.

1. The grill is a source of _____.

2. The fire is a source of _____ and _____.

3. The drum and guitar are _____.

55 Motion and Force

A Match.

1. _____ push
2. _____ stop
3. _____ pull
4. _____ speed up
5. _____ slow down
6. _____ drop
7. _____ roll
8. _____ attract

a.

b.

c.

d.

e.

f.

g.

h.

B Write.

slide   swing   wheel   magnet

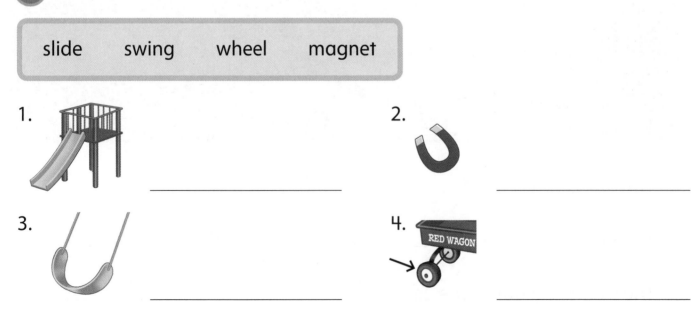

1. _____

2. _____

3. _____

4. _____

C Write.

1. The ball is _____ing.

2. It's _____ing up.

3. Now it's _____ing
   down and stopping.

D Look at the picture. Write.

1. Jimmy's mother is _____ the ball.

2. Sally's father is _____.

3. Mike's big sister _____.

A Label.

cord	plug	outlet	flashlight
light switch	light bulb	lawn mower	wire

1.

_____

5.

_____

2.

_____

6.

_____

3.

_____

7.

_____

4.

_____

8.

_____

B Write.

batteries	electricity	gas	fan

1. The car runs on _____.

2. The flashlight runs on _____.

3. The _____ runs on

_____.

C Look at the picture. Write.

1. The light bulb runs on _____.

2. The toy car _____.

3. The lawn mower _____.

135

A Match.

1. _____ guitar

2. _____ light bulb

3. _____ flashlight

4. _____ candle

5. _____ iron

a.

b.

c.

d.

e.

B Look at the chart on page 136 of the *Dictionary*. Write *heat*, *light*, or *sound*.

1. A guitar is a source of _____.

2. A light bulb is a source of _____.

3. An iron is a source of _____.

4. A flashlight is a source of _____.

5. A candle is a source of _____

   and _____.

Complete the chart.

Electricity		
	uses electricity	doesn't use electricity
light bulb		
guitar		
iron		
candle		
flashlight		

D **Look at your chart in C. Write.**

1. A light bulb uses _____.

2. A _____ doesn't use electricity.

3. An iron _____.

4. _____.

5. _____.

A Match.

1. _____ volcano

2. _____ island

3. _____ plain

4. _____ canyon

5. _____ plateau

6. _____ peninsula

7. _____ mountain

a.

b.

c.

d.

e.

f.

g.

B Label.

lake	gulf	bay

1. _____

2. _____

3. _____

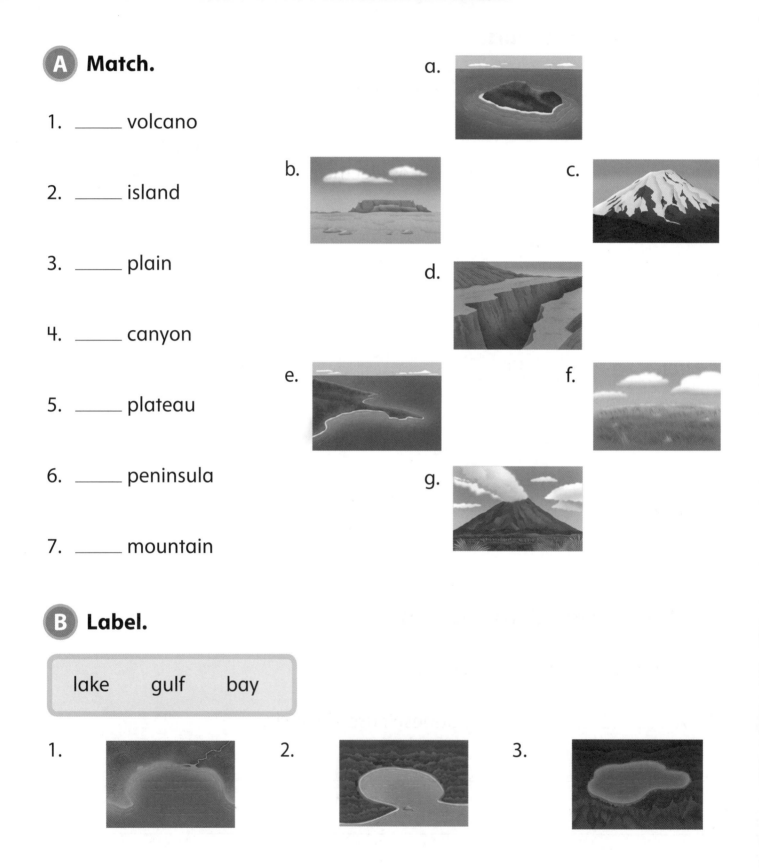

C **Write.**

1. Is a lake a landform or a body of water?

    It's a _____.

2. Is a bay a landform or a body of water?

    It's a _____.

3. Is a volcano a landform or a body of water?

    It's a _____.

D **Look at the picture. Write.**

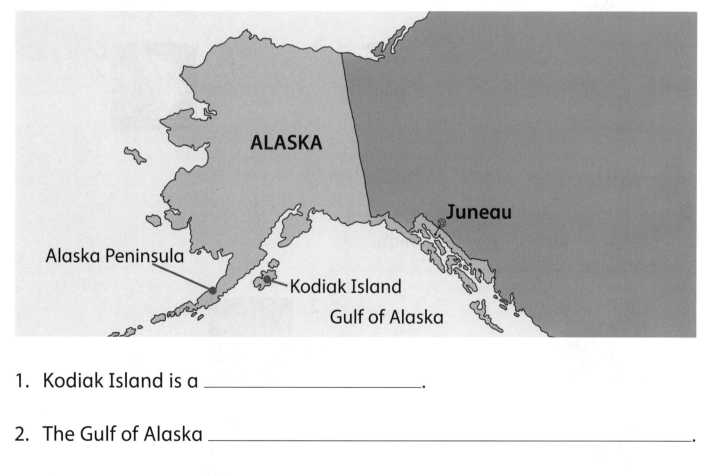

1. Kodiak Island is a _____.

2. The Gulf of Alaska _____.

3. The Alaska Peninsula _____.

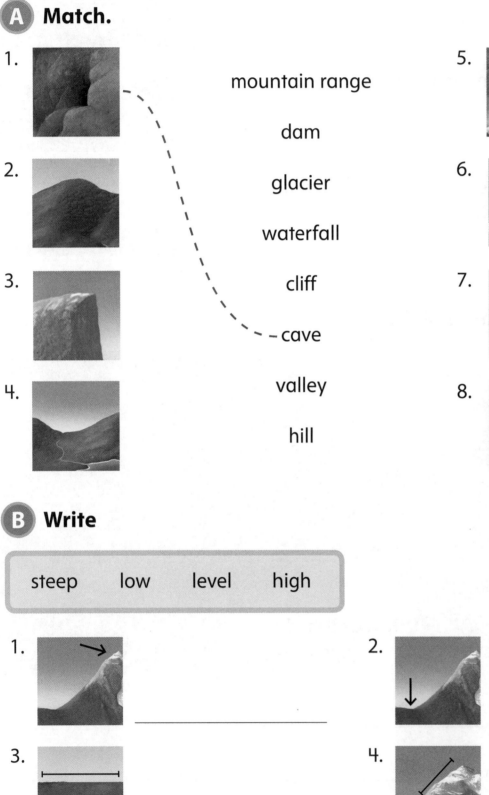

58　In the Mountains

A　Match.

1.

mountain range

dam

glacier

waterfall

cliff

cave

valley

hill

2.

3.

4.

5.

6.

7.

8.

B　Write

| steep | low | level | high |

1.

2.

3.

4.

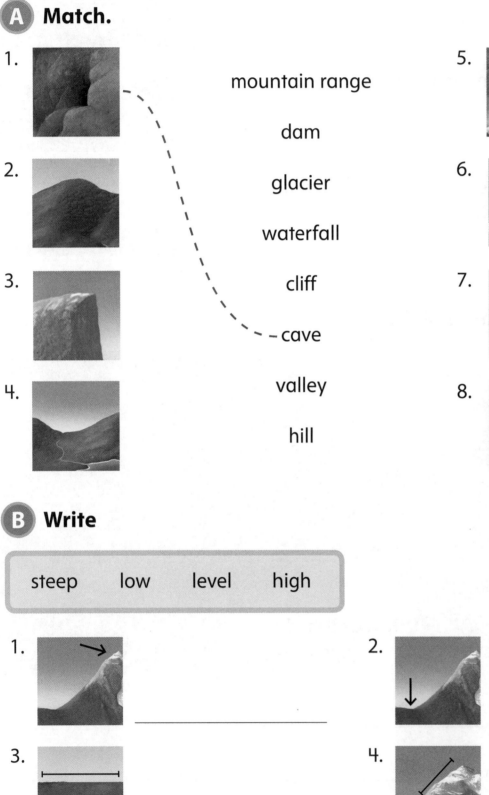

140

Write.

low	level	high

1. The valley is _____.

2. The plateau is _____.

3. The mountain range is

_____.

D **Look at the picture. Write.**

1. The glacier is _____.

2. The _____ is high.

3. _____.

A **Label.**

crystal	pebble	mud	layer	soil
clay	rocks	lava	boulder	models

1. _____

2. _____

3. _____

4. _____

5. _____

6. _____

7. _____

8. _____

9. _____

10. _____

B **Write *hard* or *soft*.**

1. The clay is _____.

2. The boulder is _____.

3. The mud is _____.

C **Look at the picture. Write.**

Soft   Hard

1. The pebble is _____.

2. The soil _____.

3. _____.

A   Match.

1. _____ skull   3. _____ horn   5. _____ footprint   7. _____ dinosaur

2. _____ skeleton   4. _____ spike   6. _____ fossil   8. _____ scientist

B   Write *meat-eater* or *plant-eater*.

1.

2.

3.

_____   _____   _____

C Write.

sharp   spikes   flat

1. Plant-eaters had _____ teeth.

2. Meat-eaters had _____ teeth.

3. Stegosaurus had _____.

D Look at the picture. Write.

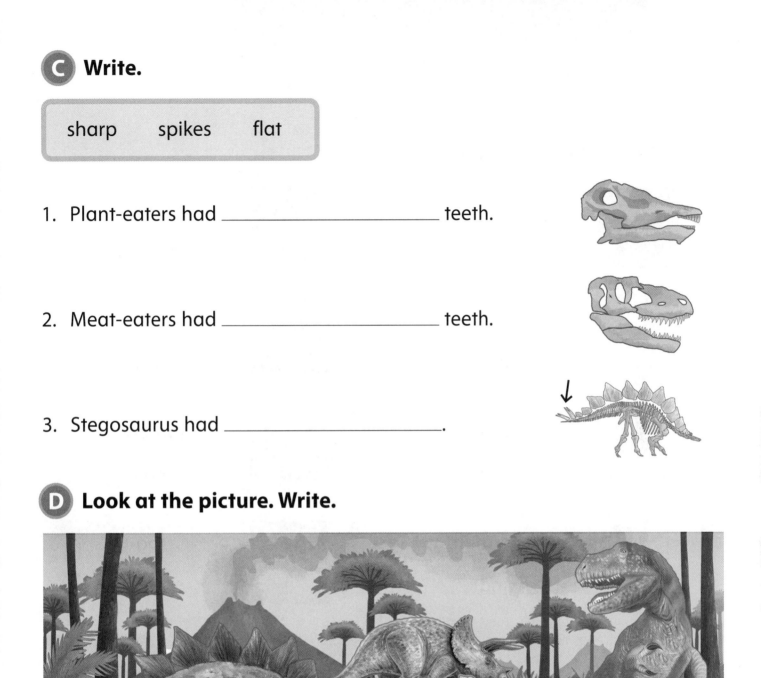

1. Tyrannosaurus rex had _____ teeth.

2. Triceratops had _____.

3. Stegosaurus _____.

A Circle the correct word.

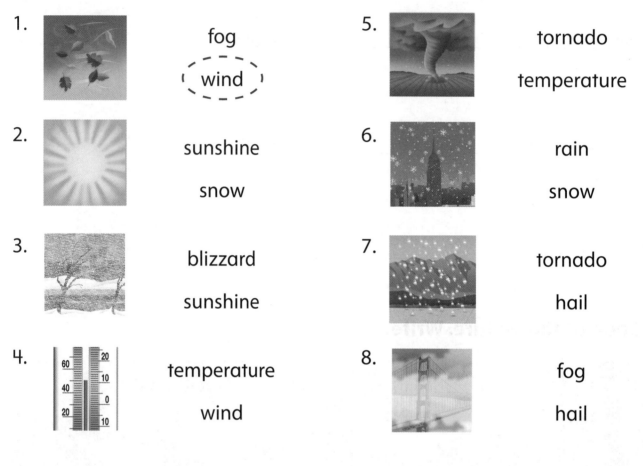

1. fog
   (wind)

2. sunshine
   snow

3. blizzard
   sunshine

4. temperature
   wind

5. tornado
   temperature

6. rain
   snow

7. tornado
   hail

8. fog
   hail

B Write.

| hurricane | rain | thunderstorm | lightning |

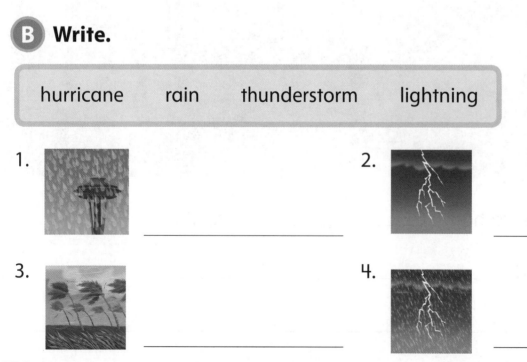

1. _____

2. _____

3. _____

4. _____

C **Write about yesterday's weather.**

1. There was a _____

   in New York.

2. There was a _____

   in Oklahoma City.

3. There was a _____

   in Los Angeles.

D **Look at the picture. Write.**

1. There was _____ in Seattle.

2. There was _____.

3. _____.

A Match.

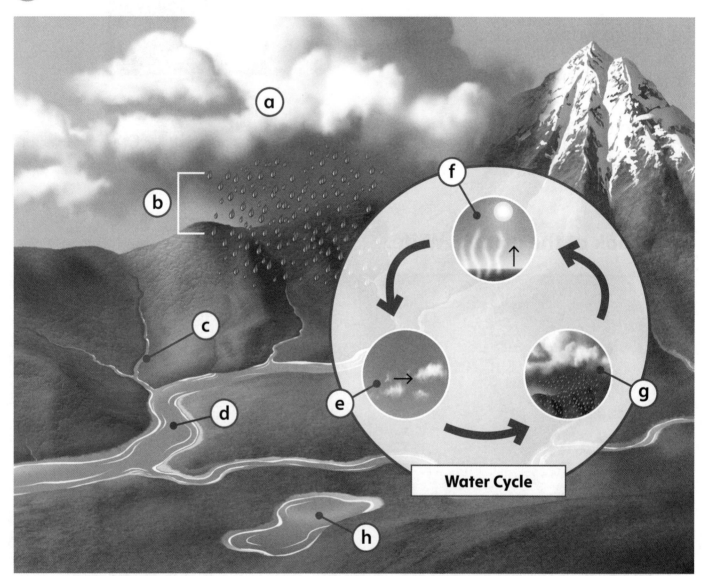

Water Cycle

1. _____ clouds

2. _____ condensation

3. _____ drops

4. _____ evaporation

5. _____ pond

6. _____ precipitation

7. _____ river

8. _____ stream

B Write.

| Precipitation | stream | ocean | lake | sea | Condensation |

1. A _____ has fresh water.

   A _____ also has fresh water.

2. A _____ has salt water.

   An _____ also has salt water.

3. _____ is part of the water cycle.

   _____ is also part of the water cycle.

C Look at the picture. Write.

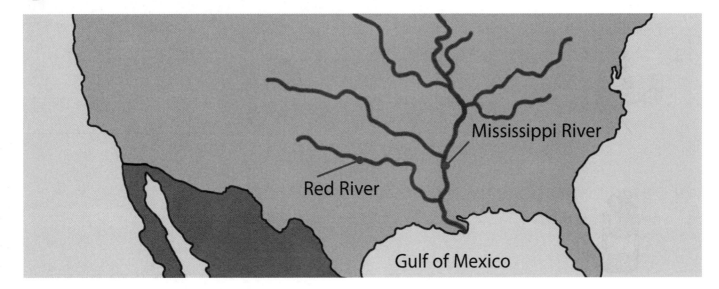

1. The Mississippi River has _____.

2. The Red River also _____.

3. The Gulf of Mexico _____.

A Label.

bins	pollution	cardboard	exhaust	glass
smog	aluminum	litter	plastic	garbage

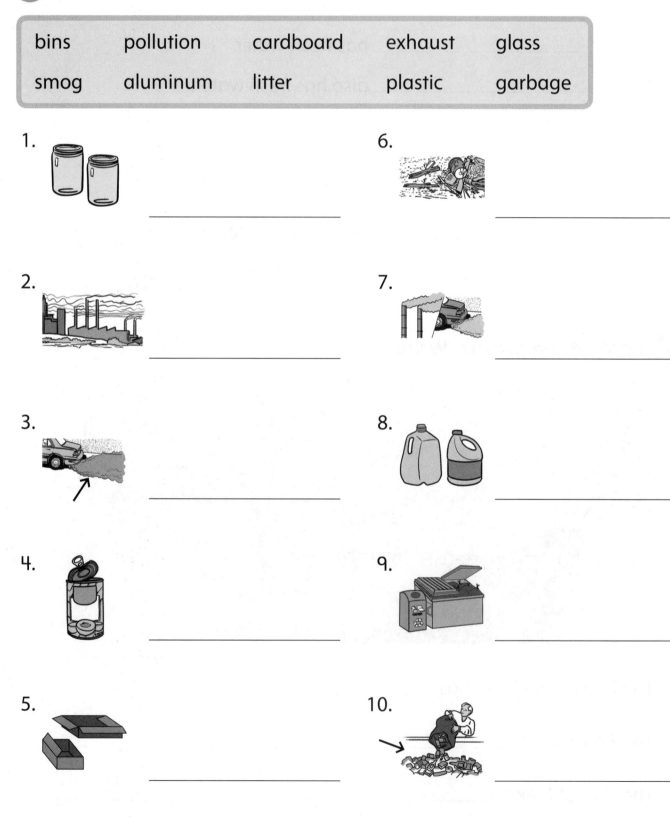

1. _____

2. _____

3. _____

4. _____

5. _____

6. _____

7. _____

8. _____

9. _____

10. _____

B Write.

recycling	picking up	throwing away

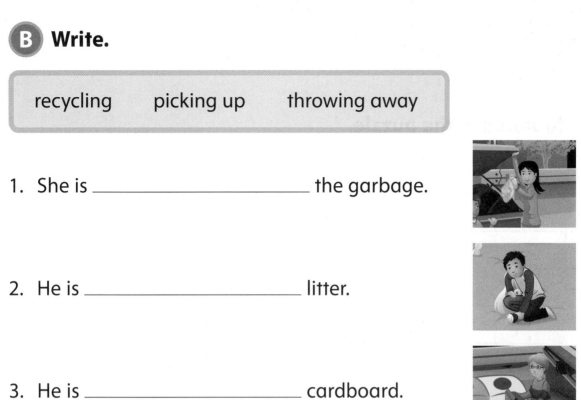

1. She is _____ the garbage.

2. He is _____ litter.

3. He is _____ cardboard.

C Look at the picture. Write.

1. They are picking up _____.

2. She is _____.

3. He _____.

A Write the words in the puzzle.

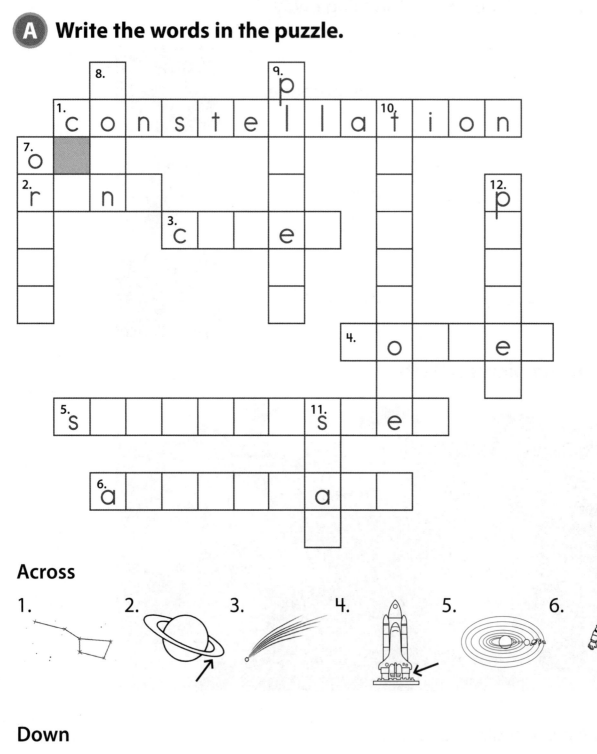

Across

1. 2. 3. 4. 5. 6.

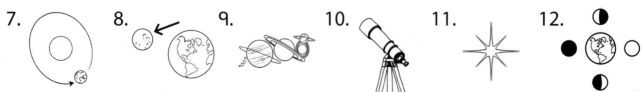

Down

7. 8. 9. 10. 11. 12.

B Answer the questions.

| star | planet | constellation |

1. What is the sun?

   The sun is a _____.

2. What is the Big Dipper?

   The Big Dipper is a _____.

3. What is Jupiter?

   Jupiter is a _____.

C Look at the picture. Write.

Space

Jupiter   Uranus
Neptune

Earth   Saturn
Venus

Mars

Mercury

1. Saturn is a _____.

2. The Earth _____.

3. _____.

A Label.

| boulder | hill | mountain | rocks |

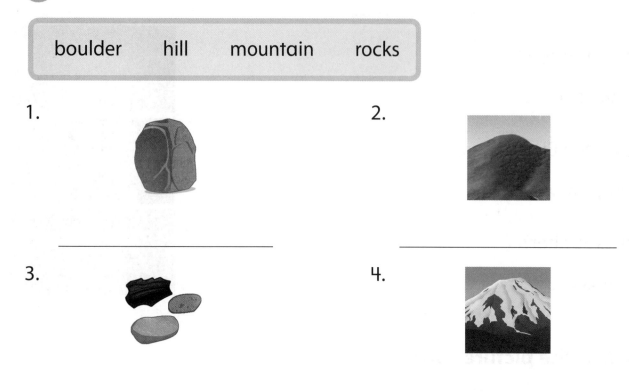

1. _____

2. _____

3. _____

4. _____

B Look at the diagram on page 154 of the *Dictionary*. Write *smaller* or *larger*.

1. A rock is _____ than a boulder.

2. A mountain is _____ than a hill.

3. A hill is _____ than a rock.

4. A boulder is _____ than a mountain.

C Complete the diagram.

gulf   lake   pond   drops

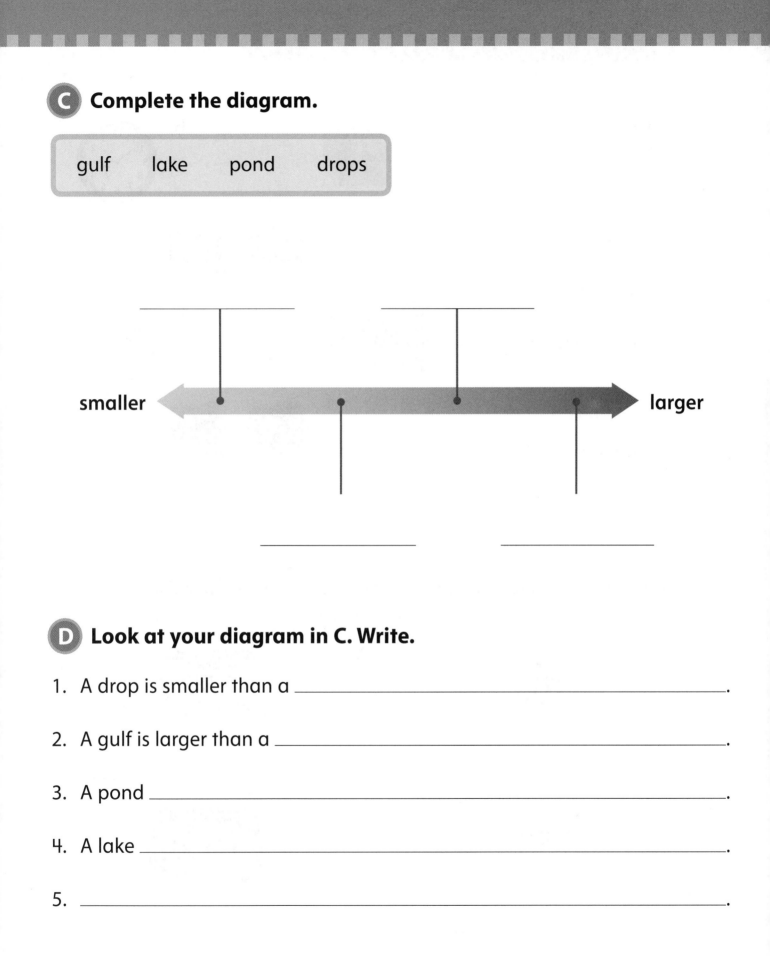

smaller ⟷ larger

D Look at your diagram in C. Write.

1. A drop is smaller than a _____.

2. A gulf is larger than a _____.

3. A pond _____.

4. A lake _____.

5. _____.

A Match.

a.

b.

1. _____ hour

2. _____ p.m.

c. 5:00 → 6:00

3. _____ hour hand

d.

e.

4. _____ minute hand

5. _____ a.m.

f. 5:00 → 5:01

6. _____ minute

B Write.

| twelve thirty | three fifteen | six o'clock | nine forty-five |

1. 3:15

_____

2. 6:00

_____

3. 9:45

_____

4. 12:30

_____

C Write.

1. The _____ is on the twelve.

2. The _____ is on the three.

3. What time is it?

   It's _____.

D Look at the picture. Write.

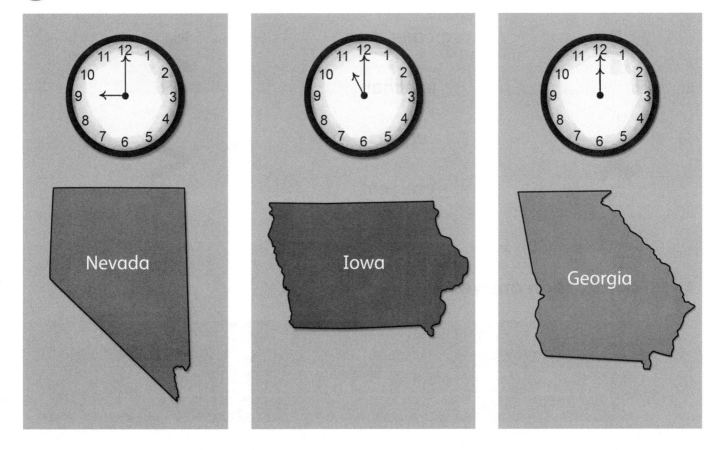

1. What time is it in Nevada? It's _____.

2. What time is it in Iowa? _____.

3. _____? _____.

A Match.

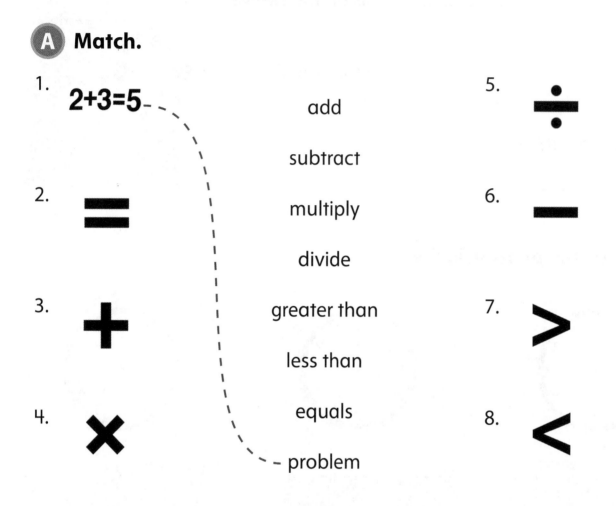

1. **2+3=5**

add

subtract

multiply

divide

greater than

less than

equals

problem

2. =

3. +

4. ✕

5. ÷

6. —

7. >

8. <

B Match. Then answer the question.

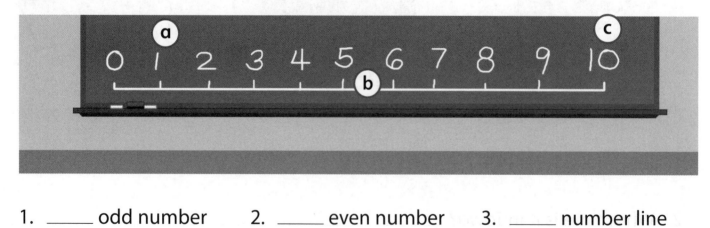

1. _____ odd number   2. _____ even number   3. _____ number line

C Write.

plus	divided by	minus	times

1. nine _____ one $9 - 1$

2. eight _____ two $8 \div 2$

3. three _____ three 3×3

4. five _____ five equals ten $5 + 5 = 10$

D Look at the pictures. Write.

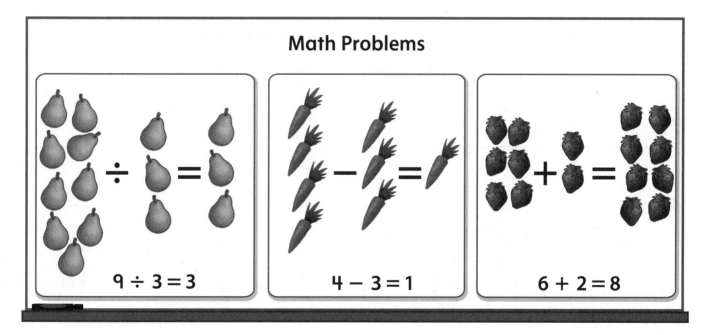

Math Problems

$9 \div 3 = 3$ $4 - 3 = 1$ $6 + 2 = 8$

1. Nine divided by three equals _____.

2. Four minus _____.

3. Six _____.

A Write the words in the puzzle.

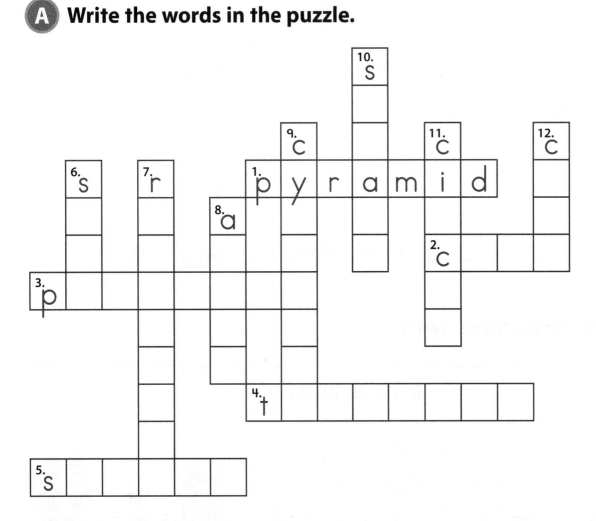

Across

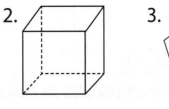

1. 2. 3. 4. 5.

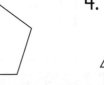 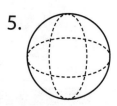

Down

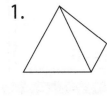

6. 7. 8. 9. 10. 11. 12.

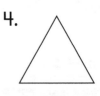

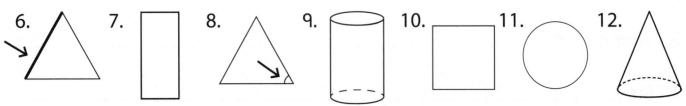

Write.

three	five	six

1. A pentagon has _____ sides.

2. A triangle has _____ sides.

3. A cube has _____ sides.

C **Look at the picture. Write.**

1. A square and a rectangle have four _____.

2. A triangle and a cylinder _____.

3. A pyramid and a _____.

A Match.

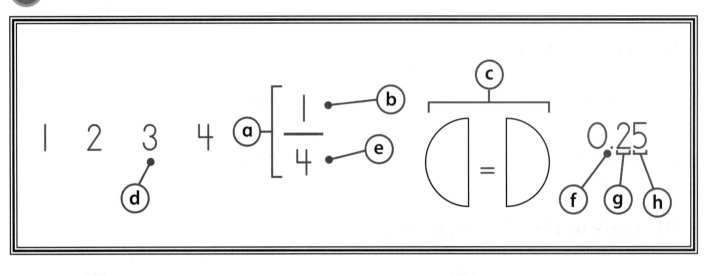

1. _____ fraction

2. _____ numerator

3. _____ whole number

4. _____ denominator

5. _____ hundredths place

6. _____ equal parts

7. _____ decimal point

8. _____ tenths place

B Label.

one half   one third   whole   one fourth

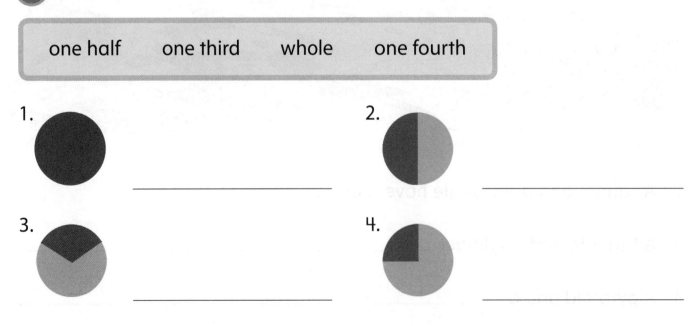

1. _____

2. _____

3. _____

4. _____

C **Write.**

1. Does she have a _____ circle?

   Yes, she does.

2. Does he have one third of a circle?

   No, he _____.

   He has a _____.

3. Does she have _____ of a circle?

   Yes, she _____.

D **Look at the picture. Write.**

1. Clara has _____ of an orange.

2. Isabel has _____.

3. Andy _____.

A Match.

1. _____ inch

2. _____ foot

3. _____ yard

4. _____ ounce

5. _____ cup

6. _____ pint

7. _____ quart

8. _____ gallon

a.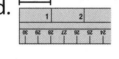

b.

c.

d.

e.

f.

g. 1 yd.

h.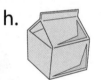

B Write.

liter	centimeter	gram	meter

1. _____

2. 1 m _____

3. 1g _____

4. _____

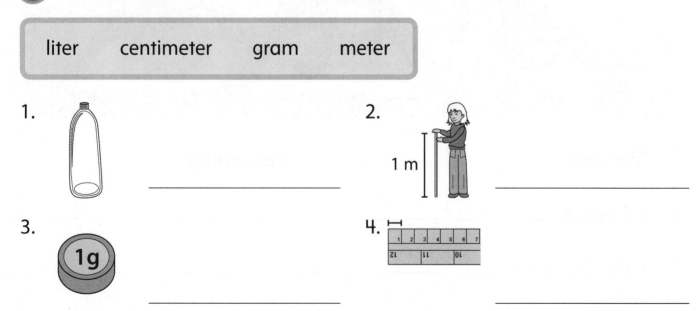

C Write.

lighter   longer   larger

1. A yard is _____ than a foot.

2. A gallon is _____ than a quart.

3. Two ounces is _____ than four ounces.

D Look at the picture. Write.

cm = centimeter
c = cup
m = meter
qt. = quart

1. Thirty centimeters is shorter than one _____.

2. A cup is _____ than _____.

3. Ten grams _____.

A Match.

1.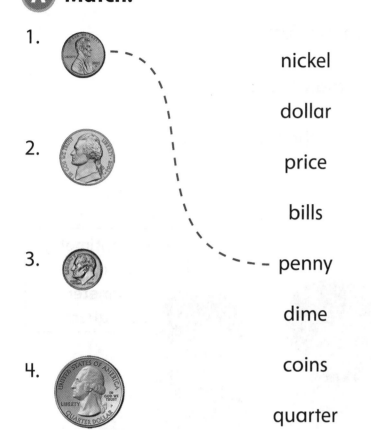

nickel

dollar

price

bills

penny

dime

coins

quarter

2.

3.

4.

5.

6.

7.

8.

5¢

B Write.

save   sell   buy

1.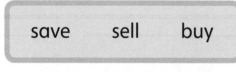

_____

2.

_____

3.

_____

166

 **Write.**

25¢	100¢	1¢

1. How much is a penny worth?

   A penny is worth _____.

2. How much is a quarter worth?

   A quarter is worth _____.

3. How much is a dollar worth?

   A dollar is worth _____.

D Look at the picture. Write.

1. Marta has one _____. It's worth _____.

2. Josh has three _____. They're _____.

3. Dan has _____ dimes. _____

   _____.

A Label.

| whole   one fourth   one half   one third |

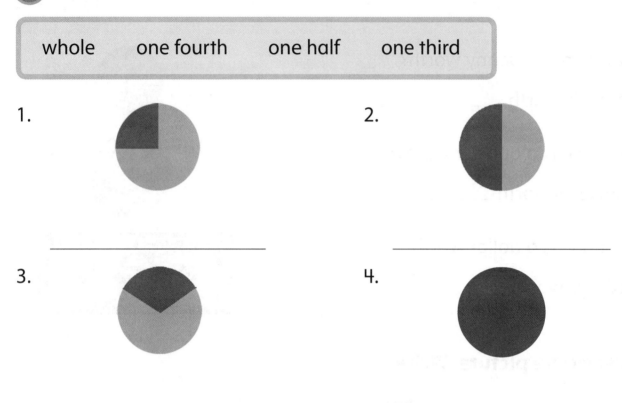

1.

_____

2.

_____

3.

_____

4.

_____

B Look at the diagram on page 168 of the *Dictionary.*
Write *less* or *more.*

1. One whole is _____ than one fourth.

2. One fourth is _____ than one half.

3. One half is _____ than one third.

4. One third is _____ than one whole.

Complete the diagram.

cup   gallon   pint   quart

less ⟵━━━━━━━━━━━━━━━━━━━━━━━⟶ more

D **Look at your diagram in C. Write.**

1. A cup is less than a _____.

2. A gallon is more than a _____.

3. A pint _____.

4. A quart _____.

5. _____.

169